The
Imposter
Within

THE IMPOSTER WITHIN

The Breakthrough Guide to Confidence, Clarity, and Living Beyond the Lies in Your Head

Garet Free

Published by Game Changer Publishing

Paperback ISBN: 978-1-968250-21-8

Hardcover ISBN: 978-1-968250-22-5

Digital ISBN: 978-1-968250-23-2

GC GAME CHANGER
PUBLISHING
www.GameChangerPublishing.com

*To all of the beautiful souls who stood by me
as I learned to build a new relationship
with my imposter within.*

*To my parents, thank you for doing your best.
I miss you.*

To my sister, I love you oh so much!

Read This First

As a thank you for buying and reading my book,
I would like to connect with you!

Scan the QR Code Here:

THE BREAKTHROUGH GUIDE
TO CONFIDENCE, CLARITY,
AND LIVING BEYOND THE
LIES IN YOUR HEAD

The Imposter Within

Garet Free

Contents

A Framework for Transformation and Lasting Confidence

U.R.G.E. – The Catalyst for Change

U – Understand yourself deeply

R – Recognize and build awareness where you're stuck

G – Get it together: take ownership and take action

E – Elevate your mindset and commit to consistent change

B.E.S.T. – Owning Your Confidence Empire

B – Build your confidence foundation

E – Expand into your full potential

S – Share your growth and impact others

T – Thrive with joy and purpose

A memorable, powerful, and action-oriented guide for stepping into lasting confidence.

Opening

Imposter syndrome isn't a syndrome.

It's a part of you that needs love, care, attention, and a gentle sense of direction instead of shame, doubt, and fear. Your "imposter self" is simply a part of you that seeks to protect you from the craziness of life and shield you from potentially unnecessary trials and tribulations.

This book provides a framework to seek understanding from your imposter self and improve your relationship with that part of you. Instead of approaching this work with the assumption that something is wrong with you, I encourage you to see this as an opportunity to get curious about why you feel the way you do.

The imposter within you is a part of you that seeks to be understood. As you work through this understanding and implement the tools for your true self to take up more space, you will discover how great it feels to be successful and confident that you deserve your seat at the table. You will shed your unhealthy relationship with luck, relish the feeling of knowing that you are enough, and release yourself from the feeling of inadequacy. Your journey has brought you here to experience freedom from the part of yourself that holds you back from being able to relax into the success of what you have achieved and will achieve.

The URGE BEST framework is a tool that I developed to provide a guide for you to improve your relationship with your imposter self. It includes the following phases:

U.R.G.E. – The Catalyst for Change

U – Understand yourself deeply

R – Recognize and build awareness of where you're stuck

G – Get it together: take ownership and take action

E – Elevate your mindset and commit to consistent change

B.E.S.T. – Owning Your Confidence Empire

B – Build your confidence foundation

E – Expand into your full potential

S – Share your growth and impact others

T – Thrive with joy and purpose

There's nothing wrong with you, but think about the opportunity to be a little bit better today than you were yesterday. Taking an intentional approach to calming the influence of your imposter self will help you on your path to leading a fulfilling life full of joy, happiness, and self-love.

I'm so excited to be a part of your journey. Now, if you're ready to change your life, let's go!

Introduction

Walking into a situation where you feel like you don't belong can be daunting. Feeling chronically inadequate despite getting the praise you deserve places an indescribable weight on your shoulders. Carrying this weight around on a daily basis takes a toll on you, your relationships, your work performance, and your overall outlook in life. It's exhausting.

Hey, I'm Garet. Having you join me on this adventure to tackle imposter syndrome (ahem, your imposter self) brings me an immense amount of joy. Having an imposter within was something that I battled with for many years without having the words for it. I learned many lessons (mostly the hard way) through my journey, and my hope for this book is that it is a tool for you to live a more purposeful and worry-free life. Writing this book is my attempt to translate concepts into action by providing you with actionable ways to improve your relationship with your imposter self.

This book is written solely from my lived experience, from interviewing others who have navigated a similar path, and from my experience managing people and coaching clients. If you're looking for a psychology or science-based book, this isn't it. This book is meant to be practical, quick, and easy to read and a reference as you work to change your relationship with your imposter self and allow your true self the space to shine brightly.

Before turning to the book itself, I feel it's important to share a bit about myself to provide context for the perspective from which it is written. My wish is that you are able to look at things more conceptually and form your own opinions as you do the work that is meaningful for your life.

My story begins in the Southeast United States. I grew up about forty-five minutes south of Atlanta in Fayetteville, Georgia, with parents who both worked at the Presbyterian church in addition to their full-time jobs. I'm a white, cis-gender, gay/queer male, and I have a younger sister.

Growing up as a gay kid of Christian parents in the South was quite the experience and probably worth a book of its own. I had a very challenging relationship with my family because much of my true self was tucked away in the shadows of my soul. It took a lot of work to discover the person I truly am and provide space for him to shine. I was not an easy kid to raise, and I fully own that and acknowledge the intricacies of family dynamics, religion, image, and everyone just doing their best.

We were solidly middle class. My parents were blessed enough to provide a house for us to grow up in where everyone had their own bedroom, and there was plenty of space so that we weren't on top of each other. We had a wooded backyard that provided a great space to play, build forts, and for me to explore on my own.

Introduction

In school, I always felt like the one who didn't quite belong. I was placed in the gifted program in elementary school around the fourth grade, but I never understood how my test scores allowed me to be there. Navigating the thoughts that LGBTQ+ kids are bombarded with from such a young age added a layer of confusion and fear inside of me that was a daily battle to navigate. Not feeling safe to discuss this with my parents or friends was gut-wrenching.

Academics seemed to come fairly naturally to me. I wasn't one who had to study much, but actually completing homework always felt like such a drag. I never understood why this was necessary. A couple of years ago, I read *Unmasking Autism* by Devon Price and pretty squarely identified with some neurodivergent traits. I've never been formally evaluated for a neurodivergent diagnosis, and I don't plan to seek one out anytime soon. Developing a deeper understanding of myself and what works for me has been the best medicine for my quirky self.

I tried soccer and track but didn't seem to do well with either. I started playing the oboe in band in the sixth grade, and that was great! I seemed to excel in music and eventually became the drum major for the marching band in high school. After drum major auditions, when the results were posted, I saw my name, and the first thing I thought was, *That can't be right.* Looking back, my imposter self was gaining momentum.

After high school, I went to emergency medical technician (EMT) school and then through my paramedic education. My first full-time job was working in a busy jail, providing healthcare to inmates. When I finished paramedic school, I started working in emergency medical services (EMS) in busy 911 systems. It was exhilarating, rewarding, and exhausting. Getting exposed to the raw aspects of humanity at a young age brought its own unique education. Being present in someone's home during some of the most emotionally charged moments of their life can be rewarding and challenging at the same time.

Eventually, I got the opportunity to work in the emergency department at a pediatric level 1 trauma center. We got the sickest of the sickest children. Working there was like learning how to swim all over again. Sick children can bring out the best and the worst in people, and I had to learn how to navigate one stressful and chaotic situation after another. Every time I was asked to go to a trauma bay, I always asked myself, *Why me?* I was great at taking care of sick kids, but my imposter self got in the way every single time. While there, I experienced some of the most challenging nights of my life, but I wouldn't trade my time there for anything.

My personal life during this time of my life wasn't that great, either. I never felt like I belonged in social situations. Dating was also quite the challenge, and I never thought that my friends really cared about me. My imposter self was having the time of his life, preventing my true self from attaining happiness. In reflecting back, I know that there was shared love with my friends during those years, but I didn't know how to receive it at the time.

After finishing undergrad and navigating some pretty serious burnout, I pivoted my career. I joined The Advisory Board Company (later Advisory Board) and found a breath of professional fresh air. While there, I found true mentors, solved fun and tough problems, and honed new skills.

However, my first couple of years there were full of negative feelings from my imposter self. Walking into the boardroom of a hospital to give a presentation instead of the ER to take care of patients led to all kinds of mental gymnastics I had to navigate. I'm beyond grateful for the professional development opportunities that were available to me at Advisory Board, like mentoring and being a mentee, learning how to be a good manager and how to do data analysis, learning about public speaking from a former news anchor, and the list could go on for quite a while.

In my more recent years, I ventured into the startup world. What I thought would be a fun time of learning and opportunities to solve interesting problems turned into a treacherous world of navigating egos and realizing that more people likely experience imposter syndrome than is realized.

I'm very lucky that I have had the space and ability to invest in myself over the last few years to identify areas that I need to work on so that my true self has full agency over me. My "imposter within" took up way too much space for far too long.

Today, my passion lies in helping entrepreneurs, executives, front-line clinicians, and businesses get unstuck, find clarity, and live with intention by unlocking their full potential and achieving lasting growth. I've traversed a long road of personal and character development, and I'm beyond grateful for the space I've had to do this work. In writing this book, I hope to provide some guidance for those looking to help their imposter selves find peace.

Creating this book presented its own unique creative hurdles and battles with my imposter self. What I came to realize is that there is a stepwise process to tackling the imposter within you. You'll find this book follows the framework that I developed to improve my relationship with my own imposter self. My intention going into this project was to be as clear and direct as possible while also producing a book that was enjoyable to read. I've tried to get to the point as quickly as possible while still filling in enough space to provide meaningful context.

Thank you for being here and allowing me to be a part of your journey. I look forward to hearing from you as you make your way through the book or once you finish.

If you'd like to work with me in my coaching program, please reach out to me at garet@theresilienceedit.com.

1

Understanding Yourself Deeply

It's January 3, 2025, as I start to write this chapter. I'm sitting in my study at home at a desk that I made for my mother when I was nineteen or twenty. This desk came back into my life last summer when it was time to sell my parents' house after both of them died. Sitting here to write a book, writing my morning pages every day (more on this later), burning incense, looking at my collection of journals, feeling the life coming from two plants, and feeling the power from big chunks of amethyst and quartz crystals that I have, reminds me of how lucky I am to be alive and able to do these things. I've learned to move through life with intention, and this writing space is intentionally curated to provide a space for creativity to flourish.

I always had a vision that I might be able to write a book, but there was also always a story in the back of my head that held me back from realizing this dream—a story with a voice from a part of me that wasn't so sure writing a book was possible. See, I wasn't a fan of writing papers in school. I was always afraid that the end product of anything I did wouldn't be perfect enough. I've always wondered, *Why me? Isn't there someone more qualified?* I just knew that somewhere along the way, someone would figure out that I didn't really know what I was doing.

Right before the idea for this book came together, I realized that I had wrestled with imposter syndrome for much of my life. I just didn't have the words to describe what I was working through. My journey through healing and repair started about six years ago. There was a lot to let go of and re-parent myself on, and patterns that needed to be identified and released.

It has been a long journey, with a lot of introspection and work on myself, including my creative self. Through all of this work, I've developed a framework that you can use as a guide to navigate your relationship with your imposter self (more on that in a minute).

Let's Get Started

Starting can often be the hardest step. As I tried to figure out the best way to start with a definition of imposter syndrome, I was feeling stuck and not sure how to proceed. My imposter self was loudly telling me that regardless of how I wrote this book, I would be labeled a fraud since I'm not an academic.

I've been in this situation before, where I get paralyzed by the need to find the perfect answer instead of finding *an* answer and getting started. I could have easily sat in the analysis paralysis mindset and watched the minutes, hours, and days tick by, but I had set deadlines for myself to get this first draft done. Overthinking wasn't an option.

Instead of trying to find the perfect way to define imposter syndrome, I asked ChatGPT. Here's what I got in response:

> **Imposter syndrome** is a psychological pattern in which an individual doubts their own skills, talents, or accomplishments and has a persistent fear of being exposed as a fraud, despite evidence of their competence. People experiencing imposter syndrome often attribute their success to luck, timing, or external factors rather than their own abilities, and they may feel undeserving of their achievements.

Common Characteristics of Imposter Syndrome:

1. **Self-Doubt:** Feeling inadequate, regardless of accomplishments.
2. **Perfectionism:** Setting excessively high standards and feeling failure even with small mistakes.
3. **Attributing Success to Luck:** Believing achievements are due to external factors rather than skill.
4. **Fear of Exposure:** Anxiety about being "found out" as not good enough.
5. **Overworking:** Compensating for perceived inadequacy by working excessively hard.

This phenomenon is often experienced by high achievers and can occur across various contexts, including work, education, and relationships.

Honestly, I couldn't have said it better myself. The words that stuck out to me the most:

- Pattern
- Doubts
- Persistent fear
- Fraud
- Luck
- Self-doubt
- Feeling inadequate
- Perfectionism
- High standards
- Overworking
- High achievers
- Various contexts

There is one word that bothers me, though: "syndrome."

To pathologize your lived experience or feelings is overkill. It's completely unnecessary to think that you were born to feel like you don't belong or deserve success.

The fields of modern psychology and psychiatry are fascinating but also full of flaws. A lot of research has been done, leading to a myriad of opinions and approaches to healing. In doing my own work, I've learned that seeking out different viewpoints will serve you well as you develop your unique worldview. When soaking up new information, I'm always curious about the origin story. Why is it the way it is today? Where did it come from? Who started this? When I started my research, I figured there must be some reference in "the literature" (a saying used in healthcare to refer to published research) to imposter syndrome, so that's where I turned next.

The concept was first discussed by clinical psychologists Pauline Rose Clance and Suzanne Imes in their paper "The Imposter Phenomenon in High-Achieving Women: Dynamics and Therapeutic Intervention." As you can see, "phenomenon" was initially used instead of "syndrome." I'm not sure if it was American society or the American medical and psychological industrial complex that transformed the initial description from imposter phenomenon into imposter syndrome, but I've learned over the years that words matter. The way we think about ourselves and others through the words we use is a determining factor in our happiness.

When it comes to imposter syndrome, it's time to drop "syndrome." We have an opportunity to rethink how we talk about imposter syndrome and to reframe it in a way that gives space for us to love, nurture, and acknowledge that part of us. Your imposter self is just a part of you, not something that is wrong with you. I invite you to join me on a journey to find better words and move through a stepwise approach to improving your relationship with your imposter self.

Your Parts

One of the best concepts I've learned about in my healing and repair journey is how we're made up of different parts. This concept has been observed in many different ways throughout the years and across cultures. As you join me on this journey to evolving your relationship with imposter syndrome, I'd like to challenge the way you think and offer tangible tools for the improvement of your relationship with your imposter self.

Indigenous or First Peoples cultures have practiced—and in many cases continue to practice—healing rituals for retrieving lost soul parts, based on the belief that trauma fragments the self. Acknowledging that ancient wisdom was doing this work prior to modern psychology is critical to moving forward with a grounded understanding of the work ahead.

In Buddhism, the self is composed of skandhas, or aggregates. The meditation and mindfulness practices in Buddhism relate to observing and working with the skandhas instead of identifying with them.

In modern psychology, thinkers and psychologists such as Sigmund Freud, Carl Jung, Roberto Assagioli, Eric Berne, Fritz Perls, Hal and Sidra Stone, and Richard Schwartz have developed theories and methodologies based on different approaches to how ego types or parts influence the self.

Richard Schwartz is known, most recently, for popularizing his Internal Family Systems approach to therapy. His book *No Bad Parts* is a great read if you'd like to understand more about how our different parts influence and make up who we are.

The knowledge that humans have different parts that make up who we are has been around for centuries. As we try to gain a deeper understanding of who we are and what makes us do what we do, we are lucky to have the ability to explore these parts in detail.

For this book, I will reference two main parts: the imposter self and your true self.

Your imposter self is the part of you that thrives on self-doubt, perfectionism, the idea that your success is attributed to luck, the fear of not being good enough, and feelings of inadequacy. Most of us are made up of many other parts, but if you have an imposter self, it may take up more space than you would like.

In my life, perfectionism has been a paralyzing struggle for longer than I can remember—to the point that it impeded my success on numerous occasions. I found myself in an ongoing cycle of creating a story in my head about a project that I needed to complete, thinking about all the ways to accomplish it, discovering everything that could go wrong along the way, imagining how that would tarnish the final product, reconsidering how to approach the project, wondering how long this was *actually* going to take me to complete, questioning how I even got there and if I was capable of doing this project, distracting myself because my mind was racing and, finally, sitting in a full-on self-doubt spiral.

All of this would happen over a few days, and before I realized it, I would have to cram everything in to meet my deadline. My imposter self was thriving, but my true self was depressed and anxious. I've lived through this pattern more times than I can count. Between school, social settings, relationships, and professional situations, I have battled with controlling the part of me that tries to hold me back from enjoying my success.

The framework in this book is how I broke free (and continue to work on a daily basis to stay free). It's not a pill, not adding a small habit to my daily life, not hoping that it would magically go away one day, but making a conscious choice to live my life in a way that is healthier for my mind, body, soul, imposter self, and, most importantly, true self. Your true self is so eager to meet daylight and shine free as you move toward achieving your dreams, one step at a time.

Your true self is the version of you that sits in the core of your body, mind, and soul. It's the peak of the mountain, the version of you that shines through when your other parts have been given the space to relax and take a back seat as it comes time for you to show up every day. Your true self is at peace, focused, and concerned about yourself before others. It communicates well and knows how to set and hold boundaries.

Stepping into my true self has been the greatest work I've ever accomplished. It has been an arduous process, full of the spectrum of emotions, but I wouldn't change the journey I've been on for anything. Finding my true self amidst the chaos that used to fill my life is the best gift I've ever given myself. I'm not perfect, and it takes work every day to maintain the space for my true self to thrive. Now that I'm aware of how it feels to have my imposter self relax and take a break, I won't be intentionally going back to giving him space to suck up energy.

Your imposter within has likely grown and developed across the years, just as your true self has. Childhood can bring numerous experiences from our parents, culture, and community that influence the growth and development of our imposter selves, just as with our true selves.

When I was in the third grade, I was bullied for the first time. A kid who went to my church and school confronted me one day using a hand gesture that I was supposed to recognize, and since I didn't, I was declared gay. The rumor quickly spread throughout my school and was the beginning of my long journey of struggling with belonging and religion and embracing my true identity. I developed a troubling relationship with self-doubt from an early age that snowballed into a full-on battle with my imposter self for decades.

Developing an understanding of what and why you feel or behave the way you do is the first step to giving your imposter within the space to relinquish control over how you show up on a daily basis. This book provides a framework to act as a guide as you navigate this work. I encourage you to be curious about how you engage with this content and relate it back to doing the work to quiet your imposter self.

Why Understanding Is Important

Have you ever had a moment of clarity where you said to yourself, *"Oh, shit! It all makes sense now"*? You can't change what you don't understand. This goes for everyone, but remember, we are all on our own journey.

Working for a pathological liar is a wild experience. I had a manager at one point in my career who was quite challenging to work for. They were consistently inconsistent. There was always a question in my mind about their motivations, and I never knew where I stood with them. My self-doubt was a raging dumpster fire because I was never sure what the next day would hold. Meetings with them were chaotic. They never followed through with what they said they would do, and I allowed their behavior to drag me down. They would say one thing, but my gut always told me there was more to the story. Their having a degree from an Ivy League school gave my imposter self even more fuel to make me feel like I didn't belong in the same space.

Without getting too specific, I caught them in a major lie one day, and it was a moment of clarity for me: there was nothing wrong with me; my manager just had a loose relationship with the truth. Finding that hard evidence showed me that regardless of your privilege, education, or background, people can still have flaws.

Reflecting on that situation, however, I wish I had understood more about what was going on within me. My imposter self was feeding on the negative energy of someone with perceived power over me, and I allowed it to happen. If I had possessed the tools to understand and acknowledge (more on acknowledging in the next chapter) my imposter within, I might have been able to release that toxic manager's control over me prior to finding proof of who they really were. I learned that there's nothing wrong with me as long as I stay true to my word.

Having words for things is critical when you want to understand and identify them. When working with your imposter within, developing an understanding of *what*, *how*, *when*, and *why* it shows up is the first step in improving your relationship with it. Knowing your imposter within intimately so that you can identify when it shows up in your daily life will give your true self the power over the part of you that sows self-doubt and feelings of inadequacy, and that tells you that you're not quite perfect enough.

When picturing my imposter self, I see a furry ogre with big paws stretched over its head to tower over me. Its breath smells, it has a slightly unpleasant body odor, and food is stuck in its teeth. In no way does my true self desire to associate with such a critter.

In my healing and repair journey, learning about my imposter within gave me the necessary understanding and words to identify when it was showing up versus my true self. Understanding this gave space for me to consciously decide which part of me showed up instead of my imposter self always taking the lead.

The work to tackle your imposter self begins with understanding where it comes from so that you can begin to find clarity on when it shows up in your life. Finding a moment of pause to take a quick inventory of which part of you is, or should be, present in any given situation is a great place to start when you're navigating a new relationship with your imposter self.

In challenging work or social situations, after doing all the work I've done, I can now (well, most of the time) take a pause when my imposter within shows up and make him take a step back while my true self has the space to lead. You have to be able to call out your imposter within, just as you would a child getting ready to touch a hot burner on a stovetop. It takes practice through conscious pauses, journaling about your day, and dissecting the narratives in your head to untangle your imposter self from your true self. Guidance from a coach or therapist can be helpful as well, but it is ultimately up to you to do the work.

Other people have an imposter within as well. As you do your work to get to know your imposter self, I encourage you to extend grace to those around you who may have a challenging relationship with their imposter within. We never know what someone else is going through, so just as you want to be extended grace, other people deserve grace from you. Grace is an amazing tool, and I'll spend more time on it in a later chapter.

We live in a world with unreasonable expectations, unimaginable stress, and people who are just doing their best. It's the perfect atmosphere for an imposter within to thrive in many of us. You can navigate through the distractions to improve the relationship with your imposter within, but it takes work. It's a journey, and if you want sustainable results, you have to dedicate time and energy to rethinking the way you show up for yourself every day.

The Birth of Your Imposter Within

Until you spend the time to identify where your behaviors and beliefs come from, you will stay stuck in the "this is how I've always done it" pattern. It's up to you to take responsibility for your true self and develop the way of living that truly serves you. Your parents raised you, but now it's your turn to make decisions for yourself.

Despite how things went down in your childhood, your parents were likely doing their best. If you were neglected or abused, there is a high chance that the behavior was the result of someone with their own unresolved trauma or imposter within. This does not excuse harmful behavior; we are still responsible for our actions. However, the ability to extend grace to the hurt child who grew into an abuser may provide you with more internal peace. If you can break free of the idea that "hard things happened to me" and move toward "hard things happened, but today I can choose how I show up," it will serve you well as you improve your relationship with your imposter within. My hope is that the remainder of this book will be a guide for you as you engage with the work of providing space for your true self to take the lead.

Growing up with deeply Christian parents was a wild ride. My parents had full-time jobs, but they both worked for the church part-time—my dad as the director of music and my mom as the organist. The church was my second home until about the age of eighteen.

For the most part, it was fine because I didn't know any different. However, once the internal battle with my sexuality started to become a more evergreen internal conversation, I started to really feel like I didn't belong and that I was an outcast. I found it hard to resonate with "the teaching of Jesus" while watching church leaders mismanage money, have affairs, lie, and treat other people with complete disregard for their internal and external struggles. My experience with the culture of Christianity is full of privilege, judgment, and discrimination.

Our early lives, the culture we grow up in, and the society around us provide the space for our imposter within to be born. The conditioning that we experience in our early years develops the part of us that regularly speaks about self-doubt and the need to be perfect, that tells us to live in fear of being found out as a fraud and that luck is the only reason we are successful, and that fuels overworking due to feelings of inadequacy. You aren't born with an imposter within. It is born from the influences in your early life that shaped you into who you are today.

Early Life

The older you get, the more you recognize moments where you're acting like one or both of your parents. While your parents were (hopefully) doing their best to provide for you and raise you the best they could, they may have unknowingly triggered the birth of your imposter self. Growing up with overly critical parents, helicopter parents, or in a home with high levels of conflict is a breeding ground for an imposter within to find its next human to settle into.

Other areas that can help your imposter within find space to be born and grow include:

- **Shame:** That first time you feel shame, especially unnecessarily, your imposter self can easily crack out of its shell and start to nurture all the negative aspects of its personality.
- **A lack of support while growing up:** If you weren't or didn't feel supported while you were growing up, I see you, and my heart aches for you. This can be a crazy-difficult feeling to navigate.
- **Having low self-esteem:** This is where an imposter within loves to grow and thrive. Kids with low self-esteem deserve so much love and care.
- **Expectations that your performance must be flawless:** This can take so much away from the experience of being a child. We are all imperfect humans, and we may grow into adults who are damn near flawless in many aspects of our lives. However, the child within us needs space to be messy and to play.
- **Parents who expect all A's on your report card:** This is a doozy and related to the above point. Putting such high expectations on a child is really a unique approach.
- **Growing up too fast:** Guilty as charged (as I look in the mirror). Instead of letting kids be kids, so much pressure is often placed on them to reach the next level. Let yourself slow down and enjoy life.
- **High pressure in academics or sports, especially if you think you're not good enough to be there:** You'll hear about my stint with soccer and track later, but it's a wild feeling to be the new kid on a sports team or

walking into a big lecture hall in college for the first time.

- **Lack of representation in your family or social groups:** Being a minority in any sense can drive your young mind wild and give space for your imposter within to grow roots.

Take a minute and let all of this settle in. If your mind starts to race with scenarios from your childhood, I invite you to pause reading and spend some time with your journal or a notebook, writing down what's going through your mind. I'll spend more time on journaling later, so you might as well begin the work now if you're having thoughts about what you've read so far.

Childhood is a complex topic. I don't pretend to have all the answers, and I acknowledge that everyone's lived experience may not align with what I've laid out in this book—not everyone has an imposter within.

Your early years and the relationship you had with your parents can be the source of so much opportunity for growth when you start your healing and repair journey. It took a long time for your imposter within to grow and develop, so it will likely take a bit of time to unravel this part of you from your true self. Leaning into the work and the desired outcome will be the fuel to keep you going.

Culture and Society

Moving through life on a daily basis can be a roller-coaster of experiences. If you aren't holed up inside your own little bubble, you likely get to experience the best and the worst of humanity on a daily basis, especially in the U.S. We've developed a society where selfishness is king, and there's a massive separation between the haves and the have-nots. Minorities experience micro- and macro-aggressions; non-minorities put their insecurities on full display when they act like they are being targeted; employers claim to be employee-focused but lay people off due to poor decisions by the C-suite; addiction is rampant across the socioeconomic spectrum; and homelessness remains an opportunity ripe for resolution. Regardless of who you are, you will be exposed to the harsh reality of modern society at some point in your life.

Your subconscious mind holds an enormous percentage of your mental power. It stores emotions, memories, events, and information that your conscious mind may not pick up on (among a lot of other functions). Moving through life in a society that is fraught with everything (and more) that I listed above, especially from an early age, can create a lot of information that feeds your imposter within.

Have you ever walked by a homeless person on payday, and the chatter in your head started to go wild? Or has someone driving a luxury car cut you off, revving up the story in your mind? Or maybe someone you love has an addiction but still manages to excel at work? All of these situations (and many, many more) will feed your imposter within if you allow them.

We can't choose our parents or where we were born. Some of us "got lucky" while others "didn't get so lucky" (according to "societal norms"). The culture of your family, neighborhood, community, and school all shape you as you grow through your early years. If you happen to be a little different from the cookie-cutter version of a human that society thinks everyone should fit into, you will face all kinds of obstacles as you grow up.

If you move from one community or country to another in childhood, the culture shock could be jarring.

If your parents divorce, you may feel lost for a while. If you have to learn a new language, it may take a long time to feel like you fit in. If your parents and family are very passionate about their way of life, they may force you in that direction as well. It can all be quite a lot for our child selves to take in and process, with much of it pushed down into our subconscious mind and away from our conscious thought. The great thing is that you have the choice to decide who you will be as you enter adulthood.

If you live in the U.S. or many other countries, you have the ability to make decisions for yourself outside of what society or your parents tell you is the right way. However, all of this conditioning from your parents and society influences you, and if those influences feel even the slightest bit sticky, your imposter within will have a joyous time creating a narrative in your conscious mind that leads to self-doubt, perfectionism, feelings of inadequacy, fear of being exposed as a fraud, and thinking that your success is due to luck because you don't deserve it.

How Your Imposter Within Grows and Thrives

Shame and success fuel your imposter within.

Regardless of how big or small a success is, your imposter within thrives on it. This may seem counterintuitive, but your imposter within loves when you're successful because then it can make you feel bad about it. You may be doing well in many, if not all, areas of your life, but on the inside, your imposter self is shaming you for your success by bringing in those feelings of self-doubt, fear, perfectionism, and inadequacy. It is a vicious cycle where you are the victim, and your imposter self is the persecutor.

Your success tries to be the rescuer, but your imposter self can easily overpower that, given the strength it has built over the years. Breaking free from this cycle takes work. Along with the framework in this book, I highly recommend *Breaking Free from the Victim Trap* by Diane Zimberoff. I reference her work a couple of times here, but recognizing when you're stuck being a victim while being persecuted by your imposter self, can help you know when it's time to step out of that cycle and work through a problem instead of just holding on to it. Otherwise, you'll stay stuck in the same pattern, continuing with a life that doesn't serve you.

Your imposter self was likely born when you were in your childhood years. Your parents, family, community, and society all influence who you are and, thus, the birth and growth of your imposter self. Nobody is born with an imposter within, and no one chooses to have an imposter within regularly dragging them down.

When you are young, you are at the mercy of your parents, family, community, and society. You are a sponge that soaks up everything around you, and you assume that's the right way. Once the wheels are set in motion, the beliefs and ways of life that are instilled in you from an early age snowball (for some people) into existential crises that have to be reconciled later in life when you're ready to define life in your own way.

Your parents did the best they could with what they had access to, so when you're ready to take the leap, you have to untangle what they taught you and rebuild yourself from the ground up. This may not be the case for every single thing your parents taught you, but you have the opportunity to revisit everything in your life to decide if it serves you or if a different version fits your true self.

My mother was very concerned with how other people perceived us growing up. I often heard, "What will other people think?" as a child for things like running across the parking lot instead of walking. I'm not sure why that was important to her, but it led me to place too much weight and control in the hands of other people when it came to my happiness. The book *The Subtle Art of Not Giving a Fuck* by Mark Manson helped me unwind some of this thinking. I had to figure out that I am responsible for my happiness and that my imposter within would love to continue to thrive on self-doubt and perfectionism unless my true self decided to take back the control and power that I had given to others—many of them people I barely even knew.

Your imposter within will thrive on your success, insecurities, and childhood beliefs until you edit your story, allow the past to be the past, and choose to live in the present in a way that honors your true self and not your imposter within.

When I was a paramedic, I took care of a newborn that weighed about five pounds. Born premature and in a fragile state, he was about six weeks old when I cared for him. He was in desperate need of IV access to give him life-saving medication, and we were trying our best to find a good vein. When a baby is that small, finding a vein that will hold an IV catheter is challenging.

After a lot of discussion with the physician, nurses, and parents, we all agreed that the only option left was to try to get an IV in his neck. He had a beautiful external jugular vein, but his neck was tiny. None of the caregivers in the room had ever put an IV in the neck of a baby that small, but we knew that this child's life depended on it. I was always proud of my IV skills, but this situation was a new frontier. The physician told me to make it happen, and I was a bit nervous. Caring for small children is a very rewarding yet challenging experience. Their parents trust you with their children's care at some of their most fragile moments.

As I considered how I would make this IV attempt successful, I gathered the necessary supplies, placed a small blanket roll under the baby's shoulders, and took several deep breaths. I prepped the skin very carefully, played with the positioning of his skin to keep the vein secure while the needle and catheter entered his neck, and asked for help to keep him secure as I executed the procedure.

My heart rate was elevated but not quite racing. I wondered what would be next if this didn't work. The story in my head was, *This vein is gorgeous, but I've never put an IV in the neck of a baby this small; am I sure that this is the right thing to do?* Another breath helped settle my mind and nerves for a minute because it was time to get this done.

After the baby was wrapped in a firm grip of love and I got everything situated just right, I punctured the infant's skin in just the right place to have the IV catheter's hub sit where I thought would be best on his tiny neck. When I saw the rush of blood come in (as it is supposed to), I was so grateful.

Taking another breath, I told myself to move thoughtfully so that I didn't fuck it up. Advancing the needle just a little bit more allowed me to unload the catheter off the needle and into the vein. It slid in like a hot knife into butter, and I knew that this was the right decision for this child to get the medications that he needed. Success!

After getting the dressing applied and everything secured, I left the room and was noticeably sweaty and a bit exhausted. Plenty of my coworkers congratulated me for doing a good job, but the narrative in the back of my head was telling me that I should have been able to get an IV in him without having to stick his neck, that I only got that IV because I was lucky, and that I'd never be able to do that kind of work again. My imposter self couldn't let me enjoy just one tiny moment of success.

The decision is yours, and either choice can be the right one. Choosing to give your imposter within space to control your outcome and outlook on life is completely acceptable. Nothing is wrong with you if you choose to live your life feeling self-doubt, leaning into perfection-ism, feeling lucky that you're successful, living in fear that you will be found out as a fraud, and overworking because you feel like you have to overcompensate for your self-imposed incompetence. You may experience more mental and physical health problems because of this choice, but again, that is your choice.

If you're interested in making a different choice, one that is more nurturing to your true self, where life feels more fulfilling and less like a chore, I invite you to keep reading. Your imposter within is probably screaming at you right now, saying that you are fine and don't need to keep reading, but I dare you to lean in and see what you can discover about yourself.

For many years, I thought I was *just* a paramedic, a cog in the wheel of the healthcare machine that no one really cared about. As a paramedic, I had high demands placed on me, but the pay never matched the expecta-tions (when I was working clinically). Such a situation can lead you to really question why you chose that path and to wonder if your needs will ever be taken care of.

Working two or three jobs at a time as a medic allowed self-doubt to live in the front of my mind. Ques-tions like:

- *"Will I ever be able to get ahead?"*
- *"Will I have to work like this for the rest of my life?"*
- *"Am I even good at what I do if I have to work so hard to pay my bills?"*
- *"When will I ever be able to save for retirement?"*

All of these questions swirled in my head for a long time, even as I was caring for a patient having a heart attack or putting an IV in a six-week-old baby in the pediatric ICU. As I worked through navigating my relationship with my imposter self, I had this moment when I realized that I had done some pretty amazing things as a paramedic.

Working in an ambulance in a busy 911 system is hard work. My first job in an ambulance was twenty-four-hour shifts, and I was making $10 an hour at twenty-one years old. That job taught me a lot and was very formative to the trajectory of my life. I'm forever grateful for the good things it taught me and for the negative experiences that taught me how to be a better human and leader.

One patient always sticks out to me. He was getting chemo, had a bad reaction, and was going into cardiac arrest. As we arrived at the infusion clinic, his breathing had just stopped, and his heart rate was quickly descending to zero. If my partner and I didn't act quickly, he would soon be dead. At twenty-one, I was in charge of saving this man's life—not the oncologist in the room (who should have been doing CPR), but me.

I now realize that I had a huge responsibility in situations like these. Making split-second decisions that have life-or-death implications can be a heavy burden to bear. This situation was no different. We quickly scooped this man up, provided the care he needed, which included CPR, intubation (breathing tube), and medications through an IV. All of this was done in the back of an ambulance with just the help of my partner and my supervisor, who showed up for a few minutes at the end. We did what needed to be done and got him to the hospital. Two weeks later, I happened to be at the hospital and saw him leaving, headed to a rehab facility to get his strength back.

In reflecting on that situation eighteen or so years later, I was amazed that twenty-one-year-old me saved someone's life. That is an honor that not many people get to hold. It was very grounding for my imposter self to acknowledge that I've been achieving greatness for a long time. It helped me step into the magnitude of my full and true self and really sit with the fact that I'm more than the work that I do or the feelings of my imposter self.

I'm a creator. An artist. A reader. A writer. An author. A devoted friend. A coach. A relationship builder. A leader. Obsessively curious. A yogi. A house (music) head. A traveler. An anthropologist. A foodie. A partner. The list could go on.

As soon as I stopped limiting myself, everything shifted. Doors opened. Confidence grew. Opportunities unfolded. I never would have guessed that I'd write a book, but without my imposter self holding me back, I created the space to execute my life's work.

Your Imposter Within in Your Adult Life

Growing up can feel like chaos wrapped in expectation, especially in today's society. One day, you're playing outside with some neighborhood kids, and the next, you're trying to figure out how to "adult," pay bills, and make money. Many of us might have felt the insecurities associated with our imposter within early in life, but it wasn't until our adult years that we found the words to describe what was going on inside our minds. Having words (and the right words, for that matter) for what you experience is important and helpful while you're working to edit your story, break patterns, and chart a new path. You can't fix what you can't name.

Imposter syndrome isn't a syndrome, a disease, a disorder, or a condition. Although psychologists may railroad me for taking this position, I welcome the healthy conversation.

As you grow into the amazing adult that you are, it is helpful to take time to introspect. Dig deep. Analyze yourself and get curious about why you act and feel the way you do. Question your behavior and decisions, specifically who the decisions are made for.

- Do you live for yourself?
- Do you live for your parents?
- Do you live for your imposter within?
- Do you live for your true self?

Since you're reading this book, you're likely curious about that part of you that shows up in your daily life to sow self-doubt, perfectionism, and feelings that your success only comes from luck. It makes you worry about being found out as a fraud and encourages you to overwork so that you can prove your worthiness.

That part of you is your imposter within. It feels the need to protect you from continued success because you may get hurt along the way. It tells you that the smallest mistake isn't acceptable, that your hard work doesn't matter, and that you're just lucky to be successful. It is the ball of stress you feel because someone may ask you something that you don't have the exact answer to in the moment, and it tells you to bury your head in your work so that people perceive you as an expert in your field.

This part of you is slowly eating away at your long-term health and happiness. It can be challenging to understand where your imposter within comes from, and you may never find the exact answer. However, you can do the work today to change the relationship with your imposter within to remove that stress from your life. As you'll see, approaching this part of you with curiosity will help to set the stage for continuing the work to live life centered on your true self.

At the end of each chapter of this book, I'll provide some journaling prompts or other activities to help you begin (or continue) to unpack your relationship with your imposter within. I invite you to use this work in a way that serves you best. Some options include:

- Complete the work as you read each chapter.
- Read the book all the way through and then complete the work for each chapter.
- Read the book with a friend, your partner, your coach, or your therapist and do the work together.
- Read the book with a group, book club style, and discuss.
- Do the work alone and then discuss it with a friend, your partner, your coach, or your therapist.
- Read the book and don't do the work.

The great thing about doing this type of introspective work is that you, your true self, are in total control. You may hear from your imposter within as it becomes fearful of what is to come, but you have to remind that part of yourself that it is safe and your true self is capable of protecting you.

Work at Your Pace

When writing or journaling, I encourage you to have a daily practice. In *The Artist's Way*, Julia Cameron requires you to write three pages every morning. I'll spend some more time on that later in this book, but for now, I encourage you to start with a similar practice to build the habit of having a physical landing place for your thoughts every morning. This will help to clear the cobwebs and give you a fresh slate to begin your day.

For the prompts below, consider if you want to write about them during your morning pages or separately. Either way, dedicate some time to thoughtfully exploring each question and allowing your thoughts to flow freely onto the paper.

1. What experiences or relationships might have contributed to my feelings of self-doubt and the need to prove myself?
2. What specific thoughts or situations trigger my feelings of self-doubt or inadequacy, and how do I typically respond to them?
3. What evidence do I have that contradicts my belief that I'm not good enough or don't deserve my success?

1. If I spoke to myself the way I speak to my best friend or partner, how would I reframe my self-doubt?
2. How would I show up in my life if I fully trusted myself and my abilities and believed that I belonged where I am?

Once you've spent some time on the above journaling prompts, reread what you've written, and then answer the prompts below:

1. What recurring themes, beliefs, or emotions came up from the above questions, and how does it all impact the way I see myself and my abilities?
2. What specific actions, habits, or mindset shifts could I take to challenge these limiting beliefs and build confidence in who I am?

When you're finished, congratulations! Taking inventory of where you're beginning is the first step to uncovering the opportunity to change your relationship with your imposter within. If you feel up for it, I'd love for you to share what you've discovered about yourself. My email address is garet@theresilienceedit.com.

The rest of this book is here for you when you're ready to continue your work, so if you're ready, keep going.

2
Recognizing Your Imposter Within and Cultivating Awareness

It wasn't until I was writing this book that I figured out that my self-doubt fuels my procrastination. I had a chance meeting with Ed Barrows on January 23, 2025. Ed is an accomplished leadership coach, professor at Brown University, and author of two books. I highly recommend that you check out his book *Twelve Skills* if you're looking to grow as a leader.

We got to chatting, and he gave me some great advice based on his experience of writing two books and working on his third: start building your audience now, prior to the release of your book. As I was walking to the gym the next day and debriefing the conversation with Ed, I had a moment of clarity that took me by surprise. My imposter within was doing his best to keep me from having a successful book launch.

Posting on social media and talking about myself have never been things that I've enjoyed. I've always allowed the attention to be on other people. During that walk to the gym, I realized that self-doubt and the need for perfectionism were holding me back from sharing what I was working on and getting my message out to those who might benefit from the work I'm doing.

I was holding back because my imposter within was trying to protect me from the potential disappointment that I could face if even one person were critical of my work. In that moment, I found an opportunity to step away from the narrative that my imposter within was scripting and be more intentional with how I approached the process of writing this book.

Ideas are great, but action is where the magic is. To quiet my imposter within on this specific situation and work toward successful results, I spent some time developing and documenting a social media strategy that would guide my work for the book outside of writing every day. Documenting is one of the key parts here. Getting my ideas out of my head and onto paper is critical to my true self controlling the outcome and preventing my imposter within from taking back the reins. Having a document to reference on a weekly basis as I develop content made all the difference in the world when it was time to share what I was working on through my social networks.

Intentionally acknowledging the situation, understanding why I thought the way I did, and quickly executing on a plan to prevent my imposter within from controlling this narrative again was the process I used to get out of my own way so that my true self could get shit done. This process is work and takes time and energy, but it is so worth it once you experience success.

Evaluating When Your Imposter Within Shows Up

How often have you entered a scenario and there's a story playing in the back of your mind, screaming about self-doubt, perfectionism, the fear of being exposed as a fraud, the belief that you'll have to overwork yourself or that the only way you'll reach success is through luck? For me, it's been more times than I can possibly count. In fact, it's a daily occurrence.

Taming your imposter within is a journey that takes time, effort, and diligence. Once you understand what your imposter within is, the next step is understanding when it may show up and push your true self to the side. From the smallest situations, like almost running into someone at the grocery store with your cart as you come around the corner, to more impactful ones, like getting up to do a presentation in a boardroom full of executives, there are countless moments when your imposter within can show up in your daily life.

Transitioning from being a paramedic into tech and consulting was a ride full of twists, turns, and rewards. I was just a few months into my tenure at Advisory Board when I was asked to present during a client meeting to a group of executives and physician leaders. Some new functionality was being rolled out for our analytics tool, and it would look at data in a way that would be new for our clients and the industry. There was a big clinical component to this, so I was tapped to deliver the message.

When it was our time to present, the moment I walked into the room, my imposter self saw the twenty-ish people in suits and lab coats sitting in a U-shaped arrangement behind tables and instantly started to do its best to

31

create a narrative in my head that could have derailed the entire presentation.

I was hit with thoughts like:

- *Who do you think you are?*
- *You are so uneducated compared to these people. They're going to figure out that you're JUST a paramedic.*
- *I bet the physicians in the room have published tons of research. Aren't you scared of them figuring out that you haven't done that level of work?*

The list could keep going, but hopefully, you get the point. That day will always be memorable because I made it through. I didn't hyperventilate or make any major mistakes. I didn't get laughed out of the room (which was a legit fear about thirty seconds after walking into this space that intimidated me).

The presentation wasn't my best work, especially compared to what I've grown into today, and I was likely far harder on myself than I should have been. What I learned is that we all have to start somewhere. Even though I was a great medic and proud of the skills I had developed as a clinician, it was time to keep going and push out of my comfort zone. I didn't have the words back then to understand the influence of my imposter self, and that's part of why I'm here with you now, putting what I've learned out in the world in the hopes that at least one person can find value from it and more rapidly improve their relationship with their imposter within.

Until a year or two ago, it was very challenging for me to accept praise or recognition. There have been countless times when someone graciously acknowledged my presence, work, or effort, only for me to be awkward because I wasn't sure how to respond. A shy "Thank you," "Oh, it's no big deal," or "That's just what I do" were common phrases that came from my mouth when someone gave me praise. I didn't know what to do because my imposter self was telling me that I could have done better, that I really didn't know what I was doing, and would be found out as a fraud. It's an exhausting headspace to live in.

After I finished emergency medical technician (EMT) school and while I was in paramedic school, I had the honor of working with a fellow EMT student who also happened to be an athletic trainer. He had just started working at a new high school and needed help with football games for the school's first season. I went to every football game, home and away, doing whatever I was asked, helping with injuries, and soaking up as much knowledge as I could from the athletic trainer side of things.

At the end of the season, I was invited to the football banquet. It was such a nice gesture, and I was happy to attend. As the head coach was passing out awards and such, he started to give a speech that was a little ominous about someone who had volunteered a lot of time to help the team get up and running over their first season. At the end, he called my name and held up a plaque to present to me.

I was floored. Having to walk to the front of that room to receive that plaque was daunting. I broke out in a cold sweat, my palms grew clammy, there was a tightness in my chest, I was not sure how to walk, and the room began to narrow in. My imposter self was taking up all the space in my head with a story about how I didn't deserve to be recognized and really hadn't done that much work. Self-doubt was alive and well.

Situations like that were a big part of what led me on my healing and repair journey. I wanted to learn how to mitigate my imposter self proactively so that I didn't have these moments where it stole the show from my true self. Not wanting to readily accept compliments or recognition was a prime example of how my imposter self was running my life. Every time a compliment came my way, self-doubt took over instead of joy.

Whatever narrative you allow to be repeated regularly in your mind will either build up or break down your true self. Self-doubt prevented me from truly acknowledging my wins and achievements so that I could build on that positive momentum to achieve greatness earlier in life. Looking back, my imposter self was thriving because I brushed off the positive reinforcement that came my way instead of using it as fuel for my true self to lead.

Now it's your turn. Have the examples I've provided sparked you to think about parts of you that may not be serving your true self? The writing prompts below are for you to work through now or whenever you're ready to begin to recognize when your imposter self may be showing up in your life.

- When do you feel most like you don't belong?
- What types of situations make you doubt yourself, your qualifications, your relationship, or the work that you've done?
- Describe in detail one situation in recent memory where your imposter within may have been taking up too much space. Get as specific as possible with all the little details

from the physical space to the narrative running in your head.

- Every day for a week, write about any time that you have felt like an imposter, felt self-doubt, felt perfectionism preventing you from taking action, felt like you're overworking, felt afraid that you are a fraud or not good enough, or felt like you hit success because of luck. At the end of the week, look for themes or how you might be able to identify your imposter within more proactively as you move forward.
- Who or what tends to amplify your feelings of self-doubt, perfectionism, overworking, fear of being a fraud, or luck driving your success?
- Recall a recent experience where you brushed off a compliment or praise for your work or an achievement. If you could relive that moment, what would you do differently?

Cultivating Awareness of Your Imposter Within

What does it mean when you get that sinking feeling in your gut, your palms get sweaty when you walk into a room, or you keep avoiding something that really must be completed?

What about recurrent fear, regular self-criticism, unnecessary perfectionism, or tension in your body?

Are you known for procrastinating, over-preparing, or being withdrawn?

All of these signs, feelings, and behaviors could be your imposter self controlling your actions.

When I was in middle school, maybe sixth or seventh grade, I was diagnosed with scoliosis. My spine curves in two places instead of each vertebra correctly stacking on top of the lower one. I'm very grateful that my posture has never been affected, but boy, have I had to deal with pain right in the middle of my back. The area just a little lower than my shoulder blades, on the right side of my spine, loves to spasm and remind me of my imperfect body.

For years, I thought this was something that I would just have to deal with, power through, and be tough about. Anytime I was stressed, my back would be in knots. There have been times when I was in so much pain that it was hard to take a breath or focus on anything other than the spasm in the middle of my back. In addition to the physical uniqueness, I eventually figured out that I hold a lot of stress in my back.

Part of my healing and repair journey led me to yoga and weightlifting. These two practices have been a game changer, not only for my mood and relationship with my imposter self but also for releasing me from regularly feeling that nearly unbearable pain in my back. We hold a lot of emotion and stress in our muscles and fascia, and I learned that much of that for me was in the middle of my back. When stress, self-doubt, or perfectionism are raging through me, my back will clench in a big, spastic knot.

Recognizing when my body is telling me that something is off and needs to be addressed was a huge step for me. I learned that stretching could help in moments of crisis with my back pain, but as I stayed curious, I found that being proactive with a regular practice was more impactful for me. When I'm in my regular flow of caring for myself, I rarely have back pain now. Caring for mind, body, and soul will allow you to release the symptoms from your imposter self through the affected area.

Awareness begins the work of creating space between you and your imposter within. Having mindful awareness puts into motion the process of uncoupling your true self from your imposter self so that the narrative of not being good enough has the space to dissipate.

The framework in this book is a stepwise approach to doing the work to release your true self from your imposter within. There's no magic wand or pill to instantly make you better. You have to do the work, so what is holding you back?

Seriously.

Take a moment and get clear on what's preventing you from doing the work to release yourself from the control of your imposter self. By now, you should know that my favorite way to do this work is by writing, but if that doesn't feel good, think about it, talk about it, or paint it. Whatever works for you and your process.

Taking the first step can often be the hardest. However, I choose to think that easing into transformative work leads to more sustainable results. Your imposter within has grown and developed over many years, so it's going to take some time to settle it down.

Starting with taking inventory when it shows up in your day-to-day life is the best way to begin. When something happens that makes you feel "crunchy," take a pause and ask yourself if that feeling has been driven by your imposter self. If the answer is even possibly yes, great! Take note of that and move on with your day. As you gain repetitions with this practice, you'll be able to add in techniques, such as taking a pause, savoring a deep breath, and giving your true self the space to take control.

Your imposter self can show up in many ways throughout your everyday life. When you are in the throes of a contentious relationship with your imposter self, you may have feelings or behave in ways that don't feel like they align with who you are. Noticing that feeling when it happens, along with what situation caused it, is critical for you to get started with untangling your imposter self from your true self.

Writing the situations down is a great tool to give those feelings a place to land and provide a reference for when you're working with a coach, therapist, or want to measure your progress on your own.

If you're not quite sure about all of this, here are some examples of behaviors that could result from your imposter self taking up too much space.

Overworking and Perfectionism: If you spend an excessive amount of time on tasks or projects because you are overpreparing or striving for flaw-lessness, I'd encourage you to notice that this is happening. Then ask yourself if you are creating this obstacle to avoid being exposed as incompe-tent, or are you trying to prevent harsh feedback?

Reframe it this way: What if you always did your best and proactively asked for feedback with the intention of getting better?

Procrastination: Do you delay getting started on a task or project due to fear of failure or not meeting expectations? Allowing this story to take up space in your mind can reinforce the feelings of inade-quacy that your imposter self thrives on.

Reframe it this way: What if you got started with a part of the whole and worked on it daily, bit by bit, until you were finished, instead of focusing on what the final product should look like?

Discounting Your Achievements: Have you attributed your success to luck, timing, or something outside of your control instead of your own competence?

Reframe it this way: What if you replaced "I'm so lucky" with "I'm so grateful"?

Avoiding Opportunities: Do you turn down new challenges like promotions or public speaking for fear of not being ready enough? Are you focused on being perfect in a new situation, or are you known for your humility and ambitious spirit as you tackle your opportunities head-on?

Reframe it this way: What if you said yes more than you said no? What if you viewed every situation as an opportunity for growth, regardless of the outcome?

Seeking Constant Validation: Are you enough, or do you rely heavily on external approval from other people to feel competent? What triggers your cycles of self-doubt?

Reframe it this way: What if you woke up every morning, looked in the mirror, told yourself, *"I love you,"* and committed to being a badass just for today?

Self-Sabotage: Do you engage in behaviors that undermine your success, like missing deadlines, underpricing work, or not advocating for yourself? What feels good about not standing up for your needs?

Reframe it this way: What if you developed healthy boundaries with yourself, your loved ones, work, alcohol, and technology?

The Comparison Game: Do you constantly measure yourself against the other people in your life? Do you tell yourself a story that everyone else is more competent or deserving than you are?

Reframe it this way: What if you took ownership of who you are–the good and the parts that you're still learning to love–and showed up in the world with as much authenticity as possible?

Shrinking Yourself: Is it normal for you to minimize your skills, knowledge, or accomplishments when someone recognizes you for the badass that you are? Is it hard for you to take up space?

Reframe it this way: What if you acknowledged that every human is equal?

Fear of Asking for Help: Do you worry that seeking guidance or assistance will expose a lack of knowledge or competence in you that will prevent your future success? Does it take you longer to get something completed because you refuse to let others in?

Reframe it this way: What if you asked for help with *everything* that you do?

Emotional Exhaustion and Burnout: Has the pressure to constantly prove yourself led to chronic stress, anxiety, depression, and burnout? Do you feel like you don't know where to turn in multiple areas of your life?

Reframe it this way: What if you allowed yourself to not have all the answers and instead gave focus to being present and listening–acknowledging without the need to respond?

That was a lot of self-reflection, so join me in taking a deep breath in your nose for four seconds and then releasing it out of your mouth for eight seconds.

Repeat it if that would feel good.

Giving a presentation to an executive audience can be nerve-wracking. When I first started presenting in these rooms, my nerves (aka my imposter self) would try their best to seize control of my heart rate, breathing, vision, and sweat glands. I had already meticulously prepared and knew that there was no reason for the presentation not to be received well. However, time and time again, I would be a nervous wreck. I may have appeared calm on the outside, but on the inside, I was wound up tight.

When I learned about approaching these situations with no expectations related to the outcome, my perspective shifted. Focusing on doing my best during the presentation instead of creating a story in my head about where the outcome was going gave me space to be present with what I was there to do instead of worrying about something that hadn't happened yet. Entering into any given situation with no expectations prevents the need to spend mental energy on worry.

In addition to no expectations, I turned to a tool from my days as a paramedic: breathing. Your breath is your life force and can hold so much power in regulating you in tense moments. Taking a deep breath and savoring a long exhale helps activate your vagus nerve and slow your heart rate down. Doing this a few times before going in to do a presentation provided space for my body to feel safe so that I could execute to the best of my ability.

The best way to use breathing to slow down is to inhale for four seconds through your nose, expanding your belly first and then letting the air fill your chest. When you think you're at the top, take in one last sip of air. Hold it for seven seconds. Then release it from your mouth slowly for eight seconds. Repeat immediately at the bottom of your release for a total of five rounds.

Are you starting to see where there may be areas of your life where your imposter self is taking up too much space or impacting you in a way that could be released?

How does it feel to know that you're not alone?

The best part is that there is light at the end of the tunnel if you keep working to give your true self space to lead.

Your Turn

Here are some more writing prompts to help you explore your imposter self. Take your time with this work. Move at a pace that feels sustainable.

- Spend some time exploring where your imposter self takes up too much space in your life to acknowledge what is happening.
- Write about a recent time when you felt that your imposter self was taking up too much space. Get as detailed as possible.
- What triggered your imposter self to show up?
- What did you feel, think, and do in those moments?
- If you had the opportunity to approach the situation differently, write about what you would do next time.
- Now, repeat the above exercise every day for a week. After the week is complete, reread what you've written.
- Write about the themes you notice. Where does your imposter self like to show up?
- Is there anything, or anyone, that triggers your imposter self to show up?

Cultivating awareness of when your imposter within shows up in your daily life is a critical step to learning how to create space for your true self to take the lead. You must be aware in order to move forward. If you want to see the benefits of your imposter within not taking up so much space, I encourage you to start leaning into this work. You are a mighty soul, and doing this work can be so rewarding.

But...

You have to start now. Take inventory so you're clear on where you're going.

3
Get It Together: Take Ownership and Take Action

Enough is enough.

Waking up hungover was a frequent occurrence for me during the period of my life before I got my shit together. Outside of work, I frequently engaged in activities centered around alcohol. The escape alcohol provided was soothing in the moment, but it had a firm bite the next day.

Too much of my time was wasted on drinking and being hungover. My true self didn't have an appreciation for how precious life is, despite being a paramedic and seeing countless lives ended at an early age. My imposter self was holding me back from processing my emotions in a sustainable way, holding me back from living my life in a way that was authentic to my true self, and slowly killing me one late weekend night at a time. I knew I had to do something different, but I was too terrified to take the leap.

Transformative work can only happen when you're truly ready for the biggest investment of your lifetime—and not one day before. You have to be ready to fully commit, think differently, and make different decisions. When embarking on your healing and repair journey, you must shed the current version of yourself as you write the new chapters of your life. To get the results that will help calm the imposter within and give your true self the space it needs to shine, you have to be ready for the ride of your life.

Getting ready for this can take some preparation. For most of my childhood, I was deathly afraid of rollercoasters. Hearing the screams of other people and the fear of something going wrong fueled my inner imposter, keeping me from letting go and getting on one. Finally, in my junior year of high school, something flipped in my brain, and I decided to kick fear in the face and get on a rollercoaster. My first ride had one of the largest drops in the U.S., and it was an exhilarating experience.

When I decided to get out of my own way, I had the time of my life.

This lesson didn't carry over into my early adult years, but the universe knew that I had more to learn.

Making the decision to change the relationship with your imposter self can be a process full of twists and turns on a path that doesn't make much sense. There's a part of you that wants more from life, but the task of figuring out where to begin feels incredibly daunting. This provides the space for your imposter within to thrive. As a protector of your emotional self, your inner imposter has only the best intentions to keep you safe from harm. Unfortunately, they don't realize that they are doing more harm than good.

So many of us are conditioned to take the comfortable route through life. We do what we're told, trust that we are on the right path, and expect that good things will come to us. We sit in the same patterns that our parents sat in and wonder why our lives don't turn out any differ-ently. There are also those of us who work hard and learn as much as we can, and when success falls into our lap, we feel awkward and out of place, asking ourselves, *"Do I really deserve this?"* Finding the words for this is the first step to breaking free from the patterns that were handed down to you and building your own approach to living life.

You've probably noted how and where your imposter self shows up in your life. Now what?

Are you ready to do something about it?

Are you ready to invest in the work required to achieve a sustainable change in your relationship with your imposter self?

It's okay to have some uncertainty. Your imposter within still has energy and will continue to work to keep you dependent upon it on a daily basis. Exploring what it could look like to have an improved relationship with your imposter within can be a great way to see if this work is the right direction for you. You should remind yourself that you will not wake up the next day and magically feel better. Consistency and steady progress is how you win. Progress is perfection.

Do You Enjoy Suffering?

All human beings suffer. This is something that you do not have any choice about. You will suffer throughout your life, but what if I told you that you have agency over *how* you suffer?

Take a pause and savor a deep breath, in through your nose and out through your mouth. Now close your eyes and savor another deep breath, once again in through your nose and out through your mouth. How are you feeling in your body? Simply take note of what you feel and where.

Now, say aloud or silently to yourself, *"I can control how I suffer."* As the words settle in, notice what you feel in your body and anything that may have changed. Sit with this feeling for a minute. When you're ready, take a few deep, cleansing breaths and release anything that came up for you. If it's helpful, take a moment and write anything down that came up or call a friend who can listen to you for a few minutes, particularly if the experience was intense.

If you haven't already done so, I invite you to take a moment and complete the exercise above.

Suffering is an amazing opportunity to identify and release emotions. Taking control over the outcome of your suffering is an excellent step toward showing your imposter self that it's time for your true self to be in charge. Acknowledging your emotions, giving them their time and place, and consciously choosing not to give your emotions control over you is some of the best work you will ever do.

I probably could (and maybe will) write an entire book on suffering because it can be such a complex topic. We are trained to be sad, mad, or angry when something doesn't go our way or we lose someone or something near and dear to our hearts, but what if you simply accepted everything at face value, acknowledging that everything happens as it is supposed to?

There is a time and a place to feel every emotion that comes up, but you don't have to give them control over your daily life. You may be thinking that this is easier said than done, and you could be right. Just as with everything involved in transforming your life, it takes practice.

When my mom died, I was in a place on my transformation journey where I was ready to put my money where my mouth was. I had been talking for a while about this concept of feeling your emotions but not giving them control, and I knew that the universe was giving me the opportunity to practice what I had been preaching.

Losing your parents brings up all kinds of emotions, and the grief journey can be tough to navigate. When my mother transitioned to whatever was next for her, I was overwhelmed by my feelings. My stomach ached because I felt like I had become an orphan before turning forty. A heaviness weighed on my shoulders from the realization that I would never hear her voice again. There was a fire in my chest, breast cancer-fueled anger in my belly, and my frustration was at an all-time high with a society that doesn't focus more on the prevention of chronic disease.

However, I also recognized that I still had *my* life to live. Choosing to sit with and release the emotions associated with her death took a lot of energy, but it was completely worth it. Deciding to feel my emotions when they came up, release them, and move on with my day made all the difference for the first year that she was no longer a regular presence in my life. I cried, sometimes sobbing, when I felt like I needed to. I'm even releasing some tears while writing this; I don't hold in my grief.

In doing the work of creating space for myself to release emotions when they arrive, I found that my relationship with suffering improved. It takes a lot of energy to suppress the outward-facing experience of your emotions, but I learned that it takes less energy to set them free. Freedom from the control of your emotions is one of the best feelings. We all have emotions, and we all have decisions to make when they arise. Do you hold them in, or do you create space for them to be released? The duration of your suffering is a choice. You have the freedom to choose how long the circumstances of life have control over you.

As I've done my work, I've learned that intentionally creating space to release my emotions in solitude is very helpful. Every other Thursday is spent as an evening for myself. I cry if I need to cry, I scream into a pillow if I need to do that, or I have a solo dance party at home if I'm full of joy. In my daily life, I have no shame if I need to release some tears while in conversation with someone. I've gone to the bathroom while at a restaurant to cry or laugh about something.

Sharing my feelings with others has also become an important way for me to release tough moments. You won't find me having a dramatic moment like you might see on some popular television shows, but you will find me having intentional conversations with the people I love or with whom I'm building community after the acute phase of my emotional reaction. Having a level-headed conversation with someone instead of being reactive in the moment shows my imposter self that there's no space for self-doubt or feeling like I don't belong. I choose to take control of a situation and deepen the relationships that are meant for me.

Why Do You Stay Stuck?

Are you tired of the same patterns? Do you regularly ask yourself, *"Why am I doing this again?"*

If the answer to either of those questions is yes, consider asking yourself about the patterns in your life. The victim trap is a prime example, but here are some other examples that may be allowing your imposter self to thrive:

- Going to the same bars every weekend
- Hitting the snooze button every morning
- Having no desire to deal with uncomfortable situations
- Binge drinking alcohol or regularly using drugs
- Drinking alcohol or using other mind-altering substances every day
- Missing deadlines
- Not responding to emails within twenty-four hours of receipt
- Always waiting for someone else to say "hello" first
- Never admitting when you're wrong
- Yelling at your partner or friends
- Lying
- Making assumptions
- Giving half-assed effort
- Regularly being indecisive or not speaking up for what you need or want
- Complaining about your problems without seeking and implementing solutions
- Being judgmental
- Failing to be in love with yourself

There are many other behaviors that can become destructive patterns. Do you see yourself in any of the patterns listed above? If not, can you identify a pattern in your life that may be holding you back?

Staying cozy in your patterns is easy. They're what you know, and they're where you've lived for a long time. It can be difficult to recognize what is happening in the moment until you make a conscious effort to do the work to break free from them. However, releasing yourself from them takes work. There's no magic pill or easy button to get unstuck from life. It is a gradual process that requires consistency to build momentum so that the obstacles can be overcome more easily day by day.

The Western approach to healing and getting unstuck (big pharma, big pharma's marketing, and convenience) doesn't work. As we are seeing, SSRIs (those antidepressant medications that so easily get prescribed) don't work long term. A pill may help you manage your symptoms for a short period of time or assist in doing some of the heavy lifting, but if you're not doing the work to get to the core of the problem and release yourself from it, you will stay stuck.

Being stuck and not knowing where to turn next can be one of the most awful feelings that you will ever experience. I was stuck for a long time, moving through my day-to-day life, going through the motions, hoping that tomorrow would be better than the shit show that was today. Finally, I reached a point where I was pretty close to rock bottom. I was in a toxic work environment, my mom was dying of breast cancer, and I wasn't clear on my life's purpose.

My life reached a tipping point when I was home alone one evening and allowed my mind to swirl into an abyss of negative thoughts and emotions. My imposter self raged through my mind, bolstering stories of not belonging and self-doubt to the point that thoughts of ending my life began to control the narrative. For the first time, I thought through a plan on how to end my life. I contemplated the response from my coworkers, family, and friends. I wondered if I would even be missed. I was in a hopeless moment.

Moments are amazing because, just as I discussed with emotions, you have the power to allow them their time and place so that they have no control over your being or outcome. However, I knew that I couldn't rally on my own, so I asked for help. Soon after my evening of hopelessness, I started therapy and rallied my closest friends for support.

A moment of hopelessness can be an amazing gift—it was for me, at least. While it wasn't fun to navigate in the present moment, it was exactly what I needed to get unstuck. I was stuck because I was convinced that I could do it all on my own. My ego and imposter self refused to ask for help for so many years, and I stayed stuck. I was too proud to admit that I didn't have all the answers, and I wasn't ready to make the big shift into tapping into the power of my true self and doing the work to recover from the symptoms of my imposter self.

The universe has this funny way of giving you what you need in the right moment. If you're open to receiving it, it will teach you what you need to learn. Staying stuck in your life is your choice. It's up to you to decide when you're ready to move forward in life, get help, and discover your true purpose. These moments may already be happening in your day-to-day life, so what are you doing with them?

Are You Overwhelmed With Feeling Like You Don't Belong?

We all deserve to sit in a feeling of belonging, where we don't feel judged, we're able to connect with people deeply, and have a community of people around us for mutual support. However, your imposter self *hates* the feeling of belonging. When your imposter self holds the power, you will be isolated, shut down, and helpless. You won't feel like you belong.

When I hear someone say, "I'm in my head," I often wonder if their imposter self is screaming the narrative that they don't belong. The tools used by your imposter within can be self-doubt, perfectionism, the fear of being discovered as a fraud, and so on, but that feeling of not belonging is what really eats you from the inside out. The steady gnawing away at your soul from feeling like you don't belong can take a toll on you in the short and long term. It will literally eat you alive.

There's no one-size-fits-all approach to managing this feeling, but the next time you feel like you don't belong, can you make a mental note of the situation and get curious about where that feeling comes from?

- Are you in your head, or is your imposter self speaking too loudly?
- What about this specific situation makes you feel unworthy?
- What is your imposter within telling you?
- Is this the first time you've felt this, or is this a recurring pattern?

If you can create some time during the same day, I invite you to write out your answers to the above questions and anything else that comes to mind. Remember, your imposter self thrives in isolation, but when you shine daylight on these moments or thoughts from your imposter self, it will slowly but surely lose power over your sense of belonging.

The Victim Doesn't Win

Your imposter within loves to exploit any weakness it can find in you. When you're navigating the early days of this work, it can be helpful to consider how the dynamics with your family, friend groups, and romantic partners influence your ability to show up as your true self.

The victim trap is one of the best concepts I learned about in my healing and repair journey, especially as I was changing my relationship with my imposter self. In *Breaking Free from the Victim Trap*, Diane Zimberoff guides you on a path to understanding the victim trap and how you can make a conscious decision to remove yourself from it.

Diane talks about the triangle of victim, rescuer, and persecutor. We often learn this pattern from our family, starting at a young age, and it continues until we decide to break free, handle the problems we face, and move on with our lives. Diane does a much better job of explaining all of this in her book. It's a quick read and one of my go-to book recommendations when working with clients.

Imagine growing up in a home where your parents argued or had fights in front of you as a child. Your mom and dad might have interchangeably played the persecutor and victim, while it was you, the child, who felt the need to come in and rescue the victim in the fight. Fast forward to today, and you witness similar behavior between two friends or with a partner. Are you looking to rescue someone or hope that someone comes to rescue you?

I was caught in the victim trap for a long time. Reading Diane's book provided so much clarity into what was going on in my family when I was growing up, my friend groups, and my professional world. As I wrapped my head around this concept and pattern, I was able to make a conscious decision to no longer play into the trap but break out of this pattern that no longer served me.

Making the conscious decision to acknowledge, be curious about, and resolve conflicts in a way that leaves everyone feeling more fulfilled instead of broken down is the work that has to be done to break out of the victim trap. We are all humans and make mistakes on a regular basis, but it's how we respond to our and others' mistakes that shows our imposter self who is in control.

If your imposter self is in the driver's seat, you may have a more emotional and reactionary response to challenging situations. If your true self is in the driver's seat, you will have the space to pause, collect your thoughts, be curious about a meaningful resolution, and approach the repair process with compassion and care. Drama, emotionally driven fights, and shutting down do not serve your true self, so if you're looking to take energy away from your imposter self, begin with how you resolve conflicts.

We are all on our own journey, and others deserve the respect and space that we would hope they would give to us. Remember the "Golden Rule" you might have learned when you were young: *do unto others as you would have them do unto you.* It can apply to many areas of your life. I had to teach myself about boundaries as part of my journey to give my true self agency over my life's outcome. Setting boundaries and allowing people the space they need for their journey are tools to help remove you from the victim trap so you can demonstrate to your imposter within that your true self is making decisions now.

Belonging Starts From Within

No one is coming to save you.

While there is nothing wrong with leading a life full of the symptoms that come from your imposter self taking up too much space, you can make different choices to release yourself from the grip of that part of you. As the title of this chapter states, take ownership of your outcome. Acknowledge your desire to change and figure out what you need from an accountability standpoint to keep you moving forward. Ultimately, however, you have to work toward the place of holding yourself accountable for doing the work on a daily basis.

Making my way through life, outcomes didn't start improving for me until I internalized accountability and showed up for myself first, consistently. Once I dedicated time and energy to a morning ritual to get my day started in an intentional way–every day–my productivity and outlook on life improved. Cultivating an environment of inner peace starts every day when you rise to start the day.

If you can't show up for yourself and do the inner work to allow your true self to be a beacon of joyful energy, you may always struggle with feeling worthy of your success. Until you acknowledge who the fuck you are, love yourself, and regularly lead with your heart, nothing else matters. No one's opinion. No one's agenda.

Stepping into your power through healing the parts of you that feed your imposter self will give you space to own every room you walk into. Grounded, authentic, and resilient confidence is sexy. Stepping away from the need to seek validation from outside sources demonstrates to yourself and others that you are sure of who you are, what you can do, and your method.

Healing, repairing, and then building your "Confidence Empire" (as discussed later in this book) will provide the space for your true self to feel an inner level of acceptance that is the foundation for belonging. When you feel like you belong in your body, you will more easily be able to navigate belonging in external spaces.

As you journey to internal belonging, the external spaces that you belong to will change. Should you choose to heal, repair, and build a Confidence Empire, you will build new relationships and release old ones. You may even want to change the way you provide for yourself and/or your family. If you commit to doing the work on a daily basis, your relationship with your family will change, and you will experience a sense of inner peace that you never thought possible.

Ask for Help

While writing this chapter, I noticed that I needed to pause and take a deep breath. I invite you to do the same. Pause. Close your eyes. Breathe deeply through your nose, pause for a second, and then release anything that you may be holding on to through your mouth. Repeat as many times as you wish.

This book isn't all "fire and brimstone," or whatever the joke is. My goal in life is to be compassionate yet direct. When I was doing my work to heal, repair, and build grounded confidence, I didn't fully understand what lay ahead for me. While I did, and do, have an amazing support system, I didn't fully grasp the intensity of the work or the loneliness that I would have to navigate.

Some of this book may be a lot to digest. My feelings won't be hurt if you need to take a pause to digest the content on a regular basis, but I do challenge you to finish it. It's not that I need you to finish what I've created; my goal is to demonstrate to you that through an intentional approach, you can discover the best version of yourself and exceed your goals.

If you're reading this book, thank you. I hope that you find value in my framework, which was developed through a lot of trial and error and hard lessons learned. If you make it through to the end but are still not sure where or how to start your own journey, please find some help from someone.

Yes, I'm a coach and would love to work with you, and there are additional resources on my website, in addition to one-on-one coaching. However, I'm not the answer for everyone. You may need a best friend, another coach, a therapist, a healer, a bodyworker, a colleague, a mentor, a stranger, an online acquaintance, or some version of support that I'm not aware of. When you feel the urge to seek help, get curious and find what works for you.

One of the hardest lessons I had to learn was how, when, and why to ask for help. For the longest time, I felt like I had to have all the answers or else people would think I didn't know what I was doing. I would be a fraud, personally and professionally. One of the best things I learned how to navigate was to set aside the shame brewing in my belly, with my imposter self stirring the pot, and open up to people. Vulnerability from my true self provided the compassion and understanding necessary for my imposter self to lose power. It's not easy, but it's some of the best work I've ever done.

Nervous System and Gut Regulation

If you've made your way to this book because you've tried numerous other approaches (talk therapy, mindset coach, neurofeedback, EMDR, etc.) and you still find yourself falling back into the same pit of despair shortly after a small breakthrough, I encourage you to take a step back and consider rethinking your approach to your healing and repair journey.

There is only a small chance that you will realize lasting change until your nervous system is regulated and your gut is in alignment. These are the two most over-looked building blocks in the traditional Western approach to personal development, therapy, and trans-formation.

If your nervous system isn't in a regulated state, you will only continue to be triggered by old traumas, and that energy will stay stuck in your body. You will continue to retraumatize yourself if you don't approach your deep work with a regulated nervous system. If you're curious about digging into this work, I recommend researching Polyvagal Theory or finding a coach or therapist who has experience in nervous system regulation. *The Body Keeps the Score* by Bessel van der Kolk helps lay a foundation of understanding on why trauma stays in our bodies and how it affects us throughout our lives until we do the work to release it.

Getting your gut right is also essential. Many of us have amino acid and other nutrient deficiencies because of the poor food choices we make or have access to. Processed foods and sugar are slowly destroying you. If you're depressed and anxious, the first thing you should do when you're ready to move past that part of your life is fix your nutrition. The majority of the serotonin (the feel-good chemical) in your body is made in your gut, so if you want to feel good, you must start by eating good foods. That is generally agreed upon to be a diet that consists mostly of protein, vegetables, and fruits, all preferably in their whole form.

You may also need to supplement your diet with specific amino acids, vitamins, and minerals that can be difficult to get otherwise. When I dug into the work of Julia Ross, author of *The Mood Cure*, it provided an easy framework for me to make adjustments to my diet and supplements. Overnight, it made a difference in my energy levels and how I felt.

Nervous system regulation and getting your gut right are such important foundations to healing and repair work that they are the first two things that I focus on with a client when we first start working together, especially for people who are ready to do something different and realize lasting change.

Commit to Consistently Doing the Work

While writing this book, I was amazed at the progress I achieved through writing consistently every day. The first draft was halfway completed within five weeks. Twenty-five thousand words on paper in that time was something that I didn't know was possible for me to achieve until I accomplished it. That was in January 2025.

I then set a goal for myself to get the first draft completed by the end of February 2025, but life got in the way. I escaped the dank Chicago winter for some sunshine and tacos in Puerto Vallarta, Mexico. The first week in PV was a bit challenging, as there was an issue with the internet where we were staying. My imposter self crept in and created this story that I didn't need to write because, *What if I needed to look up something on the internet?* The perfectionism narrative held me back from writing. That was followed by celebrating a friend's birthday over the weekend, and I quickly fell into full vacation mode. The next thing I knew, two weeks had passed without me doing any daily writing on my book.

As I was recognizing and acknowledging what was going on, I discovered a beautiful opportunity to hold myself accountable and get back to work. No one is supervising me with the writing process, and I don't have a ghostwriter, so it was up to me to bring my true self forward and get back to the consistency of tracking toward my goals on a daily basis. Once I was back in the groove of writing, I was so grateful to, once again, be giving my creator self space to shine, even though I was going to miss my self-imposed deadline.

When you're ready to live life in a different way, it is up to you to commit to the process of becoming the best version of yourself, bit by bit and day by day. The magic solution to living a life full of joy is consistently striving to be better and holding yourself accountable for doing the work. You don't have to be perfect, but you do have to focus on consistency.

However, the thing about doing this type of work is that it doesn't have to be a linear path. There will be lessons along the way that may feel like setbacks. The beauty is in focusing on the opportunity to learn instead of creating a negative outcome narrative in your mind via your imposter self. You are a human, so the process of evolving into the best version of yourself will be messy and full of ups and downs, but it will also be some of the most rewarding work you will ever accomplish.

It took a long time for your imposter self to grow, so it is going to take a while for you to untangle it from your daily life. The process in this book is just that—a process. I started with curiosity about my healing and repair journey twelve or so years before writing this book.

Changing the way I lived my life was something that I was pretty sure I wanted, but I had to go through a lot of trial and error to figure out what worked in a sustainable way. As you'll see later in this book, I'm at a place now where I can share what I've learned, and I hope that there is some value for you as you navigate your own journey.

The best lesson I've learned is that consistency is critical to anything you do. Answering emails in a timely fashion, creating in a meaningful way, returning text messages, going to the gym, eating healthy, reading to learn, and staying away from gossip are all examples of things that require consistency if you want them to deliver results.

If you want to create space for your true self to shine past your imposter self, you have to start with consistency and build on that momentum. Commit to regular progress and to learning something new about yourself and the world every day. Acknowledge when you have a momentary lapse, but don't allow it to control the narrative. Know that you are human and deserve grace, just like anyone else does. Give grace to yourself freely, but also hold yourself accountable to get back to work. Just like with compounding interest, investing in yourself makes more of an impact as you continue to do the work on a daily basis.

Your Turn

The following writing prompts offer an avenue for you to explore some of the main points of this chapter. I encourage you to spend some time writing through them and marinating on what you're discovering about yourself.

- What does suffering mean to me?
- My own suffering comes through when I...
- I suffer because...
- What patterns do I follow?
- Which patterns serve me well? Which do not serve my true self?
- What moments of my life do I want to shine daylight on so that my imposter self starts to lose control?
- A recent time where I played the victim or got stuck in the victim trap is...
- One area in my life that I can use some help with is...
- I will ask for help from _____ because...

4

Elevate Your Mindset and Commit to Consistent Change

You are not the sum of your thoughts or emotions.

Overcoming the fear of failure or the belief that good things only happen to you because of luck is difficult work. The answer lies in building confidence, and the first step to doing this is controlling your thoughts and emotions before they control you. Peeling apart the difference between the facts and the stories you tell yourself is an absolute must if you want to move through life exuding confidence and not cockiness or timidness.

What is confidence, anyway?

Confidence is built on a solid foundation of self. This uncrackable foundation gives you an explicit *why* for the way you do things. It tells you who you are, what you stand for, what you believe in, and what you expect from other people. Until the edges of your foundation are crisp, it will be painstakingly difficult to build anything lasting.

If you don't know who you are, confidence cannot exist. A journey to building confidence is just like tackling many of life's obstacles: it isn't easy, and it takes time. There's no simple switch that you can flip, no single answer, no one thing that will magically unlock confidence.

A few months ago, a friend asked me how I had become so confident. In an instant, I was swept away, as my imposter self attempted to take me down. I felt a bit uncomfortable, my heart rate increased, and I could feel waves of nervousness sweeping through my body, wanting me to get tense and freeze up. How was it that my imposter self was about to throw off all the progress I had made?

I trusted my gut, took a pause, and remembered that I don't always have to have an answer immediately ready for any and all questions lobbed my way. After taking a breath, I told them that it all boiled down to three key points:

- Confidence has built up in me over time as I have invested in myself, discovered who my true self is, and created space for him to shine.
- It requires regular work to keep it solid. Some days, my confidence isn't great, and other days, it is exceptional.
- Like love, confidence is not a finite resource. I may have more confidence in one area of my life, but I need to do some work in another area to build additional confidence.

Confidence is what you make of it. It is yours to define because it is a direct reflection of the relationship you have with yourself. A healthy relationship with yourself and your imposter within will result in a true self that is ready to own the world.

Building Your Foundation

As with anything, using a stepwise approach, building your Confidence Empire starts with a strong foundation. Being unshakable with who you are and what you want out of life is a requirement as you build your Confidence Empire.

There's no set way to find out who you are. It is a life-long process, and you have to commit to the journey if you want to discover the benefit. There are some basics that can help get you started, and when I work with clients, the following tools provide great guidance.

Everything happens as it's supposed to. For a long time, I was of the mindset that "everything happens for a reason." When I switched my thinking to "everything happens as it's supposed to," I felt a weight lift from my shoulders. Some things can't be explained. We don't need a justification or reason for how life plays out.

The deaths of both of my parents by the time I turned thirty-eight made me feel overwhelmingly like an orphan. I never imagined that this was how my life would play out, but it did. Just as I was leaning in to do a lot of repair work on the relationship with my mom, breast cancer metastasized to her brain, bones, liver, lungs, and abdomen. She died less than six months after being diagnosed.

Looking for a reason as to why she died in this way and at that time would not have served me well in my grieving process. Giving my thoughts space to swirl out of control was not an option. However, acknowledging that this was my reality and I had agency over my reality allowed me to lean into gratitude for what she had brought to my life and everything I had learned from her.

Accepting that things happen just as they are supposed to gives your imposter self a sign from your true self that there isn't space for self-doubt, worry, or fear to creep into your conscious mind. What's done is done, so how will you respond to it?

Your past made you who you are today. Examining your sense of self by evaluating how your past influences how you show up today is a great way to start practicing giving yourself grace. Once you realize that you were just doing your best with what you had available to you and that those experiences taught you lessons that you needed to move forward, you will be able to give yourself grace. We all deserve to receive as much grace as we give others.

Very few people have a perfect past. Many of us come from a path that was wrought with emotional, physical, and spiritual challenges. If you allow the sum of your past to be a chapter in the story of your life instead of the entire book, you will create space in the present moment to learn from it instead of being controlled by it. Your imposter within wants to cling to the awful parts of your past because they are familiar. As you build the foundation of your confident self, one of the first steps is to allow the past to rest where it is—a day that is no longer accessible to you.

My imposter within took up too much space for a long time because he was clinging to the past. Every (perceived) wrong decision, every (perceived) failure, and every time I thought that I said the wrong thing to someone was an opportunity for my imposter within to remind me that I wasn't good enough, that I should stop trying, and that no one would ever like me. Listening to your imposter within will get you nowhere.

Trauma is a different beast, but I do want to mention the gravity that it brings to the table. Traumatic experiences can live in your body in unimaginable ways, and releasing that trauma can be quite the adventure. Trauma is the cause of numerous physical and psychological ailments and should be a consideration for anyone navigating physical or mental health concerns. *The Body Keeps the Score* by Bessel van der Kolk, M.D., provides much more information about trauma in the body and ways to work with it, so I highly recommend it if trauma has been a part of your journey.

An additional note: The medical industrial complex doesn't place enough importance on the impact of trauma. If you are struggling with depression, anxiety, or any other mental health diagnosis, consider seeking help from those who specialize in trauma. Given that trauma lives in the body, also consider seeking out somatic work when you're ready to release your trauma history. If you've been in talk therapy for years and not making the shifts you are seeking, I'd love to talk to you about regulating your nervous system, the power of somatics, and doing trauma work. I'll also speak to the power of psychedelics later, so be on the lookout for that.

Now, back to the topic at hand...

Shifting your mindset to align with the present moment instead of clinging to what is over and done requires intention and consistency. It takes practice to remind yourself to come back to the present moment (or your breath) when a thought about the past comes up instead of going down a thought rabbit hole that doesn't serve you.

Your imposter self will fight to keep your thoughts in the past, swirling and looping about events, people, and places that have had their place in time and need to be left there. Your true self must make the conscious decision to extinguish those thoughts before they expand into an uncontrollable wildfire in your mind. The next time a thought from the past comes up, pause, take a deep breath, and focus on the here and now. Actively let go of the thought that isn't serving you.

Regardless of what happened to you, everything happens as it's supposed to. Naming your thoughts about the past and cutting them off is a great start, but you also have to change your relationship with your past. Regardless of how evil or devastating an event or time in your life was, it happened just as it was supposed to. Your imposter self will have you cling to evil and devastating aspects instead of what you learned from the event. Making the conscious decision to release the evil and devastating aspects of your past will give your true self the space to evaluate the event through the lens of opportunity for learning. This is resilience.

When you're ready to change the narrative about something from the past, start writing about everything you've learned from that event. Get clear on how what happened to you made you into who you are today. What are you grateful for from that experience? What do you still need to process?

For a number of years, I held on to so much anger and rage anytime someone would hurt my feelings. Outwardly, I was someone who wasn't fazed by much, but on the inside, it would eat me alive. Something small like an impatient driver or something bigger like an obnoxiously rude coworker—all of it would rot my heart and soul because that anger and rage had nowhere to go. Through my healing and repair work, I learned how to let all of that go in a healthy way. Someone cuts me off in traffic? I hold compassion for them because they must be in a rush to get somewhere, and I laugh it off. A rude coworker? I pause and let them know that their behavior isn't acceptable around me, or I remove myself from the situation.

I was once in a trauma bay with a trauma surgeon who was known for his foul attitude, especially in stressful situations. We were working on a patient who was in very critical condition, and in the heat of the moment, this surgeon threw a needle across the room. Regardless of whether you're in healthcare or not, I hope you know that's *never* acceptable.

For many of us in the room, that was the last straw from this man. In that moment, a noticeable silence fell. No one directly acknowledged his behavior, but there were a lot of wide eyes looking around. In a moment, everything became about the surgeon instead of the patient we were supposed to be caring for. His poor behavior ate away at me for too long, and I'm not sure why.

As I worked through releasing that situation, I learned that speaking up in moments like that is a requirement for me. I learned that holding my ground is acceptable. I learned that leaning into uncomfortable moments can actually be a place where I shine.

Taking control of your story provides space for the evil and devastating aspects of your story to reside in the past, while pulling the lessons learned into the present provides space for your true self to control your current narrative and future story. You can continue to be miserable over something that is long over, or you can accept the lessons from your past as an enormous blessing that will guide you in the here and now so that your future is as bright as possible.

Feeling like an orphan before turning forty was overwhelming. My dad died at the age of sixty-seven on March 16, 2020, the day before the U.S. shut down as the pandemic began to rage across our country. Two years later, my mom died on July 1, 2022, also at the age of sixty-seven, one day after my dad's birthday and on the same day that her dad had died a few years before.

Grieving the loss of my parents was unlike anything I had ever experienced. As we all do, I had a unique relationship with my parents. It wasn't amazing for most of my life, but I had been doing the hard work in the few years before they died to repair our relationship and have a more level playing field with them.

My healing and repair journey brought me to a place of knowing that they wouldn't be here forever, and I didn't want any regrets once they were no longer physically here. As each of them exited this world, my own world came crashing down each time. I was brought to my knees by a depth of emotion that I didn't know I could feel.

The grief from losing my parents caught me off guard, but I was able to move through much of it very quickly because of the work I had done on allowing the past to stay in the past. Instead, I focused on what I had learned, allowing it to propel me in a positive direction. Our grievances had been settled, and I accepted that everything happens as it is supposed to. In the days, months, and years that followed, I released tears when they needed to come, and I allowed the anger, frustration, and sadness to be expressed in a healthy way every time they came up.

The lessons I learned from my parents and their

deaths are numerous, but if I had to pick the top three, they would be:

- Everyone is doing their best.
- Have the difficult conversations.
- Someone else's reality doesn't have to be your reality.

My parents' deaths felt untimely. While that was something for me to work through and release, I chose not to allow it to be the central focus point. I did choose to take a hard look at myself and invest in myself in a much more intentional way. I took a critical look at the stress and stressors in my life that had led to some relationships that needed to change: my relationship with my body and how I care for it improved, the relationship with my mind and how I care for it improved. I started to live my life for me and what I wanted instead of what society said was the right way. I chose to find alignment and sustainable happiness.

Whew! As I'm writing this, I'm taking a deep, cleansing breath, and I invite you to do the same. Reliving these moments can bring up a slew of emotions, and an intentional breath helps release them and ground us in the present moment.

Not everything from the past is negative. You likely have at least a few positive experiences, despite the evil and devastation that might have occurred. These positive experiences can elicit joy and fond memories, but your imposter within can also force you to wonder why the present moment isn't like the happy past. Your imposter within wants you to think about why today isn't like your five-year-old birthday party (or another age that happened to be fun), that time that you won the science fair, or getting your learner's permit to drive.

It can be so easy to overanalyze the past and compare it to the present, but giving it space to occupy that happy time in the past instead of creeping into the present will provide the opportunity to create more happy moments in the present.

Just as with evil and devastation, joyful moments can serve you well. Thinking back on how you felt during a joyful moment can help remind you to develop and seek out those feelings again, now and in the future. Reminding yourself of the work and dedication that it may have taken to get to that joyful moment in the past can be fuel to keep you motivated as you work to achieve your goals today.

Your past can be a source of control or a source of empowerment—the choice is yours. Doing the work to remove the sludge from your mind, body, and soul will provide the clarity to move through life with your past as a helpful companion instead of an annoying neighbor.

Thoughts are just thoughts, not reality. When you accept this, you can move forward in your life. Untangling your thoughts from reality is some of the most necessary work you will ever do as you build a solid foundation in your Confidence Empire. This part of the work to manage your imposter within requires consistent practice until you move past the control that your thoughts have over you.

We are human, so naturally, thoughts come up in our conscious mind throughout the day. But what do you do with them? Do you give your thoughts power and control, or do you notice them and allow them to pass?

Managing the narrative inside your head can take a lot of work. I didn't even realize that I had so much chatter in my mind until I read *The Untethered Soul* by Michael Singer. He talks about the uninvited roommate inside your head, who lives there rent-free and takes up a lot of space. Most of the time, we don't want them there. They have a lot of opinions on everything, keep a continuous narrative going in our head, and keep us from sitting in reality in the present moment. When I read that, something clicked for me. I realized that for so many years, my thoughts had controlled me. Thought loops, rabbit holes, incessant chatter, and doomsday scenarios had played through my head nonstop, contributing to my depression and anxiety for many years.

As I've done the work in my healing and repair journey, here's what I've learned about the thoughts running through my head (most often from my imposter self):

- **Most of these thoughts are lies.**
- **Your imposter within will do everything in its power to prevent you from being vulnerable,** but vulnerability is just the medicine it needs to relax and take a back seat. If I'm really pressed about a thought related to someone else, I'll simply ask them about it. Those conversations start with "I'm telling myself this story that..." Then I go into detail about the thoughts that were running through my head or the story that my imposter within created. Most times, I'm corrected and given the truth. Sometimes, it's confirmed that I was right. Either way, the thought is addressed and put to bed. Brené Brown goes into this in much more detail, so I highly

recommend reading her book *Dare to Lead,* or listening to her podcasts.

- **Actively managing your thoughts will go a long way toward helping you move past them.** I learned this skill from Singer's *The Untethered Soul.* When a thought arrives that you'd like to release, close your eyes, breathe in, and imagine that in your mind you're packaging it up in a pretty box (and I like to add a tight bow). Then, as you exhale, imagine that you're allowing that packaged-up thought to flow from your mind, down into your chest, and out of your body through your heart space.

When I first learned this skill, I thought it was beyond goofy. However, after some practice, I discovered that it makes a difference. I was driving one day and had a flashback from when I was a paramedic to a teenage patient I cared for who died. Instead of spiraling into a pit of despair, I used this technique of releasing the thought. I had been practicing this for a while, but this was the first time that I instantly felt better after using it. It felt so good to finally see progress.

- **Meditation, movement, and morning pages will help you proactively manage your thoughts.** Meditation for calming. Movement for release. Morning pages for a landing space. As I incorporated these three tools into my daily life, it took me quite a while to recognize why they are so important to many people. However, they are now requirements for me every day. Going to the gym six out of seven mornings (at a minimum) every week, meditating or sitting in silence every morning, and writing three pages in a notebook every morning helps me approach every day with a clean slate, excited for what's to come.

When thoughts have a way to move through and out of your body, it's much easier for them to lose their control over you. Your imposter self would prefer for you to stay at home on the couch so that its opinions can take precedence in your mind. Actively working to release your true self from your imposter self takes the work of movement, meditation, and writing.

- **Your thoughts will always be there, but you choose how to respond to them.** Life is about choices. You can continue to live just the way you are today, and there is nothing wrong with that. You can also choose to do the work and be a little bit better today than you were yesterday. Choosing how you respond to your thoughts is completely up to you. I've chosen to proactively manage my thoughts through meditation, morning pages, and movement. I also know that I have the additional tools to manage thoughts mentioned above—releasing them and being vulnerable—when my proactive tools aren't enough.

This works for me, and it may work for you. However, I invite you to continue to explore what your approach is by being curious. The only way you will be successful with this type of work is if you do it yourself. A coach, therapist, or trusted friend can be a helpful guide, but ultimately, it is up to you.

How you manage your thoughts is a powerful testament to the level of control you have over your life. If you can control your thoughts, you will be unstoppable.

Defining your values is a very helpful exercise to discover what truly guides you toward a fulfilling and happy life, and it's one of the most important steps in building your confidence foundation. It's one thing to be able to list off a few values that you've always felt aligned with, but have you ever intentionally evaluated your values and arrived at your top two guiding values?

Something has to guide your decision making if you are looking to live a life of purpose and meaning that also brings you joy and confidence. In my experience, decisions that are made in alignment with your values will fast-track you to personal happiness and success.

Value is defined in the Oxford English Dictionary as "a person's principles or standards of behavior; one's judgment of what is important in life." A value can be a big piece of your character, a way that you live life, something that is critical for you to have relationships with others, or something that is necessary for your daily life. It may seem a little silly at first, as many of us will think to ourselves, *Oh, I'm a good person.* I had the same thought when I first started to do this work. I was taking Bodhi Calagna's Creative Insight Journey class for the first time, where they had us work through an exercise to get to our top five values. It seemed a little silly, but I was also in the early stages of my healing and repair journey.

Fast forward to a couple of years ago, when I was reading Brené Brown's book *Dare to Lead*, and lo and behold, I came across a section on values. I was happy to see that Brené thought of values much the same way that

Bodhi did, but Brené encouraged the reader to get down to their top two values. Going through this exercise this time forced me to think in a very different way and spend a bit more time figuring out what was most important for me.

Both times I've done this exercise, I've been provided a long list of values to choose from. Working through the list, it is easy at first to cross off values that can be combined with one that is more important to you, or that quickly feels tertiary or quaternary when you first read them. However, working through those last few passes of the values to get down to the top two values can take some time and quite a lot of thought.

While working through this exercise, I found myself really thinking about what was more important to me and why. *How would I explain this to someone else? Can one of these values be combined into this other one that feels a little more important to me? Will I ever be able to get down to two?*

After some contemplation and navigating a few scenarios, I got down to the values of joy and truth. I figured that if a situation or decision didn't align with those two values, I'd be better off without it in my life. When I did this exercise during the writing of this book, I got down to love and integrity. I find it really beautiful how our values can evolve yet still be tied to one another.

If you're ready to identify your top two values, then scan the QR code at the beginning or end of this book or head over to my website (www.garetfree.com) and get your free values worksheet. It will provide additional guidance on working to find your top two values. Dedicate at least twenty minutes to working through the worksheet. Go through the worksheet intentionally and when you don't have anything else pressing on your to-do list.

Remember that these are *your* values and not someone else's, so as you're moving through the exercise, focus on the ones that are most important to you. Once you arrive at the two that feel right, write them on a sticky note and place it where you will see it on a daily basis. Keep it there as long as it feels good to do so.

When you're moving through your day-to-day life, start to think about how what you're doing and the decisions you make align with your values. Observe before you make changes, but the ultimate goal is for your life to be in full alignment with your values.

Self-love is critical to building a strong foundation for your Confidence Empire. If you are not madly in love with yourself, you will find it challenging to develop a confident sense of self. Feeling inadequate, like you don't belong, and that you're a failure even after small mistakes, believing achievements are due to luck instead of your skills, having anxiety about being "found out" as not being good enough, and compensating for your internal inadequacy by working to the point of burnout will never leave you until you work on the relationship with yourself and fall madly in love with yourself.

Something magical shifts in your core (soul, spirit, mindset, subconscious, or any of the other ways to think about this) when you make the conscious decision to put yourself first and love yourself. When you love yourself enough to put yourself first, you create the space to shed the beliefs that don't serve you. When you do the work to get your shit together, you demonstrate to yourself that you matter, you are capable, and you deserve all the amazing things that come to you.

Working on your relationship with yourself is a lifelong

process, just as with any relationship. It wasn't until a couple of years ago that I discovered the opportunity to fall in love with myself. I had to sit with a lot of introspection, evaluate what served me and what didn't, do the work to show myself that I matter, and find a new alignment for my life that serves me first and others second.

A great place to start with this work is to look yourself dead in the eye in your bathroom mirror every morning and say, "I love you," ten times. Do this slowly, methodically, and intentionally. You may not believe it at first, and that's okay. You now know what you need to work on. Doing this regularly may produce some surprising results, as you should eventually find that a smile starts to come to your face by the end. Keep going, and you should start to see the smile creep in earlier and earlier when you show up for yourself in the mirror every morning. Getting your day started by telling yourself that you love *you* (with repeated practice) will bring countless positive ripples throughout your day.

In my journey to self-love, I begrudgingly decided to try the "I love you" practice. I was at a point where I would try anything if it might help me feel better about myself. Looking at myself in the eye in the mirror those first few days was awkward and uncomfortable, and I could feel my heart start to beat faster, as there was a buzzing feeling in my chest. It was clear to me that looking into my own soul, acknowledging the love that I have for myself, and receiving that love was an opportunity for me to do some work on improving things in my relationship with myself.

Keeping the "I love you"s in my morning routine for a couple of months showed me that it's okay to accept myself for who I am. It showed me that if I can start the day loving myself, then life's obstacles will be much easier to navigate. This practice gave me the courage to continue to find the walls within myself that needed to be broken down so that my true self would have the space to shine brightly and take control.

Self-love is a journey, and looking yourself in the mirror and saying, "I love you," ten times won't fix all of your problems. Self-love, just as with any other love, requires work and commitment. Falling in love with yourself is part of what's required to build your solid confidence foundation. Be curious. Write about why you do or don't love yourself. What needs to change? Ask people close to you about their relationship with themselves. Shed the things that aren't working and lean into trying new things that will nurture your inner self.

Having a good relationship with yourself is a huge step in building your confidence foundation. It can be so easy in today's society to get swept away into the lives of other people or caring for others so much that we completely forget that the relationship with ourselves is the first one we ever had.

As you get your shit together and you start to invest in yourself, you should start to see that the way you treat yourself determines your happiness and how you show up in the world. You deserve happiness and to feel good about yourself, but you're not going to wake up one day and magically feel amazing. There's no medication or magic pill that will fix your relationship with yourself.

No one is coming to save you.

You have to put in the work and the long hours on yourself holistically to build your Confidence Empire and keep your imposter within in check. Being intentional with caring for your mind, body, and soul on a daily basis is the best place to start. Different things work for different people, but I've listed some general considerations below that have some ancient wisdom and/or modern science to back up their benefits. When you're really ready to invest in yourself, I suggest that you find a coach or therapist, have a discussion with your healthcare provider, work with a trainer and nutritionist, and think about making smart decisions as to how you do this work.

The way you communicate matters. Vulnerable, honest, transparent, direct, and compassionate communication will carry you a long way in finding alignment with your life and building a solid foundation for your Confidence Empire. Listening to "sit with" what someone says instead of developing your response is just as important.

As you build the foundation for your Confidence Empire, I invite you to take a critical look at the way you engage with people through conversation.

- Do you speak more than you listen?
- Do you create time to digest what they've said?
- Do you ask them questions?
- Do you start with your intention for the conversation?
- Are you talking so much that you rarely take a breath?
- Are you so quiet that people wonder if you're alive?

Finding your voice is a very helpful step in building your Confidence Empire. Dale Carnegie's book *How to Win Friends and Influence People* is a great place to start. It was originally written for door-to-door salespeople in the early 1900s, so keep that in mind as you read it. My biggest takeaway from the book is that people love to talk about themselves, so ask them questions to get them talking if you can't think of anything else to discuss. Show interest in who they are, and who cares if they reciprocate.

When it's time for a stressful, difficult, or crucial conversation with someone, your delivery speaks volumes to your relationship with confidence.

In my journey, I've learned that it's best to prepare ahead of time for a difficult conversation. Write down exactly what you want to say.

- Start with gratitude.
- Speak to the issue and how it made you feel.
- Share what you need from the other person to move forward.
- End with more gratitude.
- Give them the option to respond now or take some time to digest what you've said and come back together at a later date.

When you're having a difficult conversation, try to take as much emotion out of it as possible.

"I'm angry with you" is very different from "I had a lot of anger toward you when this happened, and that's not what I want our relationship to be centered on."

When I have these types of conversations, I try to prepare at least two to three days ahead of time. This gives me space to review my prepared notes, practice what I will say, and process and release any emotion tied to the conversation. This allows me to be as level-headed as possible when the time comes to deliver.

Sometimes this goes really well, and you're able to

have a great moment of repair so that you can both move forward. Other times, it goes poorly. I once worked with someone more senior than me who was involved in helping to mediate a situation I'd had with one of my peers. The situation involved a moment where I felt blind-sided and incredibly embarrassed in front of a client due to my peer's behavior. To remedy the situation, I wanted space to let my peer know how their actions had made me feel. My intention was to share this so that, hopefully, they would navigate these situations with a bit more finesse in the future. However, the second it got awkward with me saying, "You made me feel," my peer flipped out, and the more senior leader shut down the conversation.

It felt like they weren't ready for that level of vulnera-bility, and I held on to that conversation for far too long–allowing their reactions to influence my happiness. In hindsight, I should have moved on with my day and allowed them to continue on their journey. I could have also said something more like, "I felt (some type of way)," so that I wasn't putting my peer on the defensive from the get-go. This was a reminder that situations like this are ripe for growth and learning.

That was an example of a moment that forced me to be curious about getting out of my own way so that other people didn't influence my happiness. My imposter within had far too much control over me in this situation. However, the next time something like this happens, I will pause and rely on what I've learned instead of investing so much of my happiness in someone else's behavior.

For Your Mind, Body, and Soul

This section on self-care was initially going to be sepa-rated into different sections for mind, body, and soul.

Then I had a moment of clarity that when I'm at my best, I'm leading my life with my mind, body, and soul fully connected. The list below is a great starting place for you as you consider the direction you'd like to go with building your confidence foundation. However, there are so many resources available for everything that I briefly share here, including some in the additional reading section of this book, so please be curious as you step through this work. I've found each of these tools to be helpful in my work, but I encourage you to stay curious and find what works for you.

Yoga is one of the best things that I have added to my self-care routine. My imposter within held me back from going to my first yoga class for a long time, but conquering that fear of not knowing how to get into a pose or move like I was supposed to was one of the best things that I ever did for myself.

Yoga isn't just about movement. Yes, the movement helps to stretch your body in an intentional way that feels amazing. You are flushing your lymph system and getting to deeper layers of muscles and fascia that often don't get attention due to the fact that we are so sedentary. You hold a lot of emotion in your body, and yoga is a tool to help release it. The first time I cried in a yoga class is one of the most liberating memories I have.

The broader practice of ashtanga yoga has eight limbs or principles and practices.

- *Yama*: Ethical guidelines or moral codes, including non-violence, truthfulness, non-stealing, control over senses, and non-possessiveness.

- *Niyama*: Self-discipline, including internal and external cleanliness, contentment, perseverance, self-study, and surrendering to a higher power.
- *Asana*: Posture, which is what most of us think of when we think of yoga.
- *Pranayama*: Breath control where intention is placed behind controlling the breath to regulate your prana or life force.
- *Pratyahara*: Withdrawal of the senses so that you can turn inward and focus on yourself.
- *Dharana*: Concentration on a single thought or object so that you build stamina for meditation.
- *Dhyana*: Meditation, or sustained and uninterrupted Dharana or concentration.
- S*amadhi*: Liberation, where you experience unity with all that is. This is enlightenment.

This year, as I write this book, I plan to go deeper with my yoga practice and likely take a yoga instructor class. Not one of the classes that feeds into corporate and capitalistic yoga brands, but one that provides a balanced understanding of why this ancient practice has been around for so long.

Walking, running, or having some cardio in your routine is essential. Moving your body is a good thing, so get this in. For those who work from home, add a twenty-minute walk to your calendar every morning. Remember learning about Newton's first law of motion? If you are in motion, you will stay in motion. In my later years, I want to stay in motion. Being sedentary kills your body, mind, and soul, so start small and grow with moving throughout the day.

Meditation has been around for centuries. Regularly practicing meditation has provided the space for my internal chatter to relax and for me to connect with a deeper part of myself. Meditation has helped me develop my sense of awareness and focus on the present moment. This centuries-old practice is available to you at any moment of the day, but if you're not sure where to begin, try the Insight Timer app. A lot of it is free, and it is great for people who are curious about adding this practice into their daily lives.

Morning pages will change your life. The concept comes from *The Artist's Way* by Julia Cameron, and it's the practice of starting your day by writing three pages in a notebook or journal. These are handwritten pages. You never share them with anyone, and if you don't know what to write, you write, *"I don't know what to write,"* until something comes up.

This practice may seem daunting at first. I started journaling many years ago but never had any consistency, and thus, I never saw the benefit. The structure that Julia provides with Morning Pages, however, was exactly what I needed so that I could develop this tool as part of my morning ritual. Morning Pages helped unlock so much of my creativity; specifically, this book would never have happened without my dedication to Morning Pages every day.

While writing this, on January 9, 2025, I was having a weird morning where my energy was off and I couldn't find focus. Just prior to sitting down for my dedicated writing time for this book, I did my Morning Pages. I discovered several things that I needed to adjust and work on in my daily life, like honing my evening ritual, and I felt lighter, more focused, and ready to tackle crossing the ten-thousand-word mark with this book.

I like the large (5" x 8.25") Moleskine notebook because it provides enough space in three pages to push out the chatter in my head and get to the meaningful "unlocks" that help me be successful on a daily basis. Having a physical place for your thoughts to land helps prevent thought loops and is a tool to work through solving problems on your own.

If you're anxious about getting started, there's a section in the back of this book dedicated to prompts for your writing. In addition to prompts, think about your pages as a stream of consciousness where you simply write out everything as it comes to your mind. If writing three pages every day feels daunting, start with one, but you might surprise yourself if you commit to three pages.

Resistance and weight training have numerous health benefits. Lifting three times a week can produce major benefits for your short- and long-term health, like increasing muscle mass, decreasing fat, and increasing bone density. The higher your muscle mass as you age, the better chance you have of not having to deal with chronic illness. Too many people accept that chronic disease is just a part of aging, but I challenge you to push that narrative to the side and get to the gym on a regular basis. It makes for an excellent insurance policy. As you step into this work, be very curious and educate yourself on how to engage safely to prevent injury. If you want to be healthy as you age, start lifting weights.

Massage and body scrubs are not just a luxury. Bodywork offers so many benefits, like helping to move emotion out of your muscles and fascia, keeping your skin (your largest organ) bright and healthy, and providing you with a dedicated moment when you can relax and feel good. Think about incorporating this into your life regularly and in a manageable way.

Professional body work is great, but other options are available, too. Can you give yourself a foot massage? Can you buy a $40 massage gun from the internet and share it with your partner or family, trading massages with each other? Can you make your own salt scrub and scrub yourself down in the shower a couple of times a week? Get curious and figure out other ways to love on and pamper yourself regularly.

Skin care, especially the skin on your face, is a must as you work to put the best version of yourself out into the world. Your face is the first thing people see when you enter their field of vision, so why not keep it as bright as possible? If skin care is new to you, I'd encourage you to read *Fatal Conveniences* by Darin Olien. Darin's book gives an overview of the unknown chemicals that end up in the products we consume and use, including what is known about their short- and long-term effects on us.

When I began caring for my skin regularly, the random compliments that I started getting fueled my desire to keep up this practice. Strangers telling you how bright you look, how great your skin looks, or that you look very fresh, simply feels good. It shows me that putting effort into myself makes a difference in how people view me, and when people view me in a positive way, that feels good. When it comes to skin care, do your research, ask for help at a reputable store (like Blue Mercury), and figure out what works for you. Start small and work up from there so that you're not overwhelmed as you get started.

Manicures and pedicures are another way to influence how you show up in the world. We've all seen (or been) the nail-biters—the ones who take out their anxious energy on their fingernails instead of in more productive ways. We've also seen people with rough-looking nails.

Regardless of the type of work you do, your hands and feet deserve love and attention. The occasional (or regular) manicure and pedicure will go a long way toward preventing you from worrying about how someone may view your appearance. If you don't want to pay someone, do it yourself. Good-looking hands and feet will help eliminate insecurities so that your true self has the space it deserves to shine every day.

Nutrition is a big one, and I don't have enough space in this book to get into a lot of detail on the subject. Just like resistance and weight training, what you put in your mouth deserves research and attention to detail. You should be giving space to educating yourself about how you feed yourself.

I acknowledge that socioeconomic factors play a huge role in what and how many people eat. What I came to learn, though, is that nutrition can be about making better choices. Eating better will help you feel better and give you the focus necessary to build your Confidence Empire.

When my mom was diagnosed with breast cancer, I dove deep into researching how food affects health outcomes. There's a lot of data and opinions out there. What I decided works for me is a diet of mostly whole foods, with lots of plants, minimal processed foods or foods that come with ingredients, and minimal processed sugar. I drink filtered water, tea, and black coffee. I rarely drink alcohol because it is a neurotoxin. I've counted calories before, but I understand that the quality of those calories (hey macros!) is incredibly important.

Focusing on the way you eat as a lifestyle choice versus crash dieting to lose a few pounds will always serve you better. If you're looking to lose weight, you have to remember that it took a while to gain the weight you have, so it will take a while to shed it.

My relationship with food has been a tricky one for most of my life. What I've learned is that making a conscious decision about what I eat every single time I put food in my mouth has helped me drastically improve that relationship. Food is our fuel. If you want to feel good and have the energy to keep your imposter within in check, you have to be conscious about how you fuel your body.

Sleep will make or break you. Speaking from firsthand experience, good sleep is such a joy, but not sleeping well creates unnecessary weight for you to carry for days to come. My relationship with sleep has been one of the hardest nuts for me to crack. I have to be incredibly diligent with the way I care for myself to ensure that I get good sleep.

I've learned that movement throughout the day (plus or minus ten thousand steps daily, yoga, resistance training, and cardio), morning ritual (meditation, morning pages, stretching, and lots of water), my evening ritual (sleepy-time tea, taking contacts out two hours before bed, no screens one hour before bed, and a journal entry on my accomplishments for the day, opportunities from the day, and what I'm excited for tomorrow), and maintaining a consistent sleep-wake schedule have made a huge difference for me in the quality and quantity of sleep I get.

There are plenty of resources out there on sleep, so if this is an area where you need to improve, I invite you to get curious and start exploring what works for you.

Reading can be a game changer. We live in a society where we are consuming on a regular basis, but what is the quality of what we consume? Are you mindlessly watching television and doom-scrolling social media as an escape, or do you turn to books to better yourself and learn something new?

I didn't get into reading until I was well into my adult years. It took a bit before reading became a major player in how I spend my time each day, but I can't imagine my life without it now. As you'll see in the next section, looking at life through the lens of someone else's perspective is a helpful way to check your ego and imposter within. Approaching someone else's point of view or their story with an open mind, absorbing what they've written at your own pace, and considering how that influences your life can be a powerful way to consume. Inciting deep thinking through reading instead of frequent bursts of dopamine from your doom-scrolling will serve you well.

Create instead of being an average consumer. We are all artists and creators at heart, and discovering your inner creator will bring clarity to your life. I have thought for many years that I had a book in me and that maybe I would become a writer someday. It wasn't until I worked through *The Artist's Way* by Julia Cameron that I created the space for the creator part of my true self to do his thing. As I've gotten out of my own way, I've been able to lean into sharing what I've learned—more on this in a future chapter.

I've learned that creating is very personal. You get the choice to define how you create. Is it cooking or baking something new in the kitchen? Is it writing a poem? Is it building a new deck outside of your back door? Is it writing a book? Is it painting? Is it knitting? There are boundless opportunities in this world for your creator self to explore. As you build the foundation of your Confidence Empire, explore what feels good to your creator self. Try, fail, learn, and repeat the process until you find success.

Play is one of the first ways that we learned. As children, play was the center of our universe and, therefore, one of the ways we learned early lessons. Sharing, caring, recovering, accepting loss, enjoying a win, making independent decisions, facing the consequences of those decisions, and the magic of discovery were all lessons we learned as playful kids.

At some point, many of us decided to, or were forced to, detach ourselves from play, get serious (likely in school), and begin seeking the agenda that society tells us is necessary for success: excel at school > go to college > get a good-paying job > work too much > keep working so that you can spend more > consider retiring > finally retire > be too tired to do anything else > die.

As you build the foundation of your Confidence Empire, I challenge you to get curious about how play can re-enter your life on a regular basis. Something as simple as a board game or card game once a week is a great place to start. If community-based sports sound more intriguing, go for it. Playing catch in the park? Great. Frolicking on the beach? Do it. Having a pillow fight with your bestie or your partner? Yes.

Life is too short to be serious all the time. As the Joker said in one of the Batman movies, "Why so serious?" Let your hair down and seek out those moments in life that bring you laughter, joy, and connection.

Vulnerability will change your life. Let go of your ego and be honest with people. When I worked at Advisory Board, one of our firm's values was radical candor. We were honest and direct with each other, but also compassionate. Experiencing this in a professional setting was pretty new to me because I came from the trenches in healthcare, where survival was based on an "eat your young" and "survival of the fittest" mentality. When I learned how to let my walls down, trust people, and take ownership for my outcome through vulnerability, big shifts happened for me, not only in my professional life but in my personal life as well.

When you're ready to invite vulnerability into your life, start small and slow. Begin with those closest to you so that you learn what it's like to build a safe container. Share just enough, but not too much, and allow space for what you say to be received. As you practice this, you will get better and can open the aperture of who you are vulnerable with to a wider audience.

Honesty will serve you better than you expect as you embrace this journey to build your Confidence Empire. It doesn't matter who you are, where you come from, the level of education you have, where you got that education, or who you think you are, if you have a loose relationship with the truth, to the point that it's a character trait that other people may use as a defining characteristic for you, there is a problem.

Living your life anchored to being an honest human will open karmic doors that you didn't even know were closed. The old saying, "The truth shall set you free," holds so much access to the path of freeing yourself from the weight that you carry when you aren't being honest with yourself and other people in your life. When you start to anchor your life in honesty, you will feel lighter and more eager to push yourself to the next level.

Get rid of clutter. Clutter destroys you one bit of stuff at a time, so get rid of it if it isn't serving you or a distinct purpose. The way you keep your home and other physical spaces, such as your car, is a direct reflection of your relationship with yourself. If you're feeling stuck in the slightest, the clutter in your home could be a big source of sludge that needs to be resolved.

- Are your closets neat and organized?
- Are your kitchen cabinets tidy so that it's easy to find things?
- Do you regularly wear the clothes in your closet based on the season?
- Are the contents of your refrigerator and freezer still edible?
- Are the self-care products in your bathroom organized and easy to find?
- Are your floors clean and your carpets vacuumed?

There's no judgment if not, because I've been in a place where I wouldn't have had positive answers to all of those questions. As Tara Schuster says in *Glow in the F*cking Dark*, keep your house "dinner party" ready. My rule when I'm decluttering (usually twice a year) is to ask myself if I've used a particular item in the last year or if I plan to use it in the next year. If the answer is no to both of those, I ask myself if the item holds sentimental value or would be hard to replace. If I can't quickly justify why I have something in my house, it's time to donate it.

As you move through the process of elevating your mindset, celebrate your small wins and reward yourself. The work to calm your imposter self doesn't have to always feel laborious and daunting. There can be moments of celebration and joy, so make sure to schedule them in your calendar as you create success.

Psychedelic-Assisted Healing

Psychedelics are powerful and catalytic tools that help you sort out the challenging parts of yourself so that you can navigate a clearer path forward. As we are in the middle of a renaissance of these medicines, it's important to note that civilizations have been using plant medicines such as psilocybin mushrooms, ayahuasca, and ibogaine for centuries before the United States led the charge on the war on drugs.

These medicines have safely helped people move through trauma and into more joy-filled lives for centuries through the magic that happens in the mind, body, and soul on a psychedelic journey. The medicine has a keen way of taking you where you need to go so that you have insight into what you need to work on, release, and move through. The medicine will take you to the door and open it, but it is up to you to walk through it. My time as a paramedic was rewarding but also presented a lot of opportunities for me to release emotion that I held onto for much too long.

It was 3 a.m. and time for yet another resuscitation. A young teenager this time. His young body, lifeless. Eyes blank. Death had found him some time ago, and it was time to call it.

"Time of death, 3:28 a.m."

Ten or fifteen minutes later, his mom arrived in the trauma bay. We were standing in a brightly lit and sterile room; my nervous system was still trying to come down from attempting to resuscitate her son. She was composed yet tearful, a slight tremor in her hands. I placed my hand on her back in a frail attempt to provide some level of solace in what I'm sure was the worst night of her life. This child that she gave birth to, raised, and watched grow into a young man. Dead. Gone in an instant.

"You can have him back, Lord. His time with me is done. Thank you for blessing me with him for the last thirteen years. He's yours to take back."

Listening to her genuine and deep love for him gripped my heart in a way that I hadn't experienced before. Her presence was palpable the second she walked into the trauma bay. I quickly felt the connection she had with her son. It was deep, meaningful, and powerful. As she began speaking to her son, tears came to my eyes as I held space for her and this unexpected grief that had been thrust upon her in the wee hours of the morning. This was unusual for me. *"Crying?"* I said to myself, *"You've done this numerous times, pull it together!"*.

It could have been that in the last week and a half, I cared for six other kids who died. I had never experienced anything like it, and in this moment, when I was doing my best to show love and care to a devastated mother, I was falling apart. I didn't realize it at the time, but I had reached my capacity for this level of stress and emotion. I was overwhelmed.

Ask any paramedic about the first dead child they had to care for, and I bet that every one of them will be able to give you all of the details surrounding that pivotal event in their career. Choosing this line of work was a selfless decision made when I was a teenager, not much older than that mother's son. I had no idea the emotional toll it would take on me.

When I left the room, wiping tears from my face, my coworkers looked around at me, not sure how to respond. I was always so composed, taking care of the worst of the worst with an appearance that it didn't bother me. I quickly brushed off my coworkers, wiped my face, and got back to work. Like I was always expected to do. Like I always tried my best to do.

There were other family members who cycled through to say their goodbyes and began their grieving process.

As the family began to trickle out, it was time for the emotions to be set aside and the logistics to be handled. This early teenager, who was full of life just a few hours ago, was now cold and starting to get stiff. The color was drained from him as he transitioned from vibrant being to corpse. I could only imagine what was going through his mother's head. Could she have prevented this? What will life be like without him? Is she still a mother? Is this her only child? Can she afford to bury her child? Will she feel guilty for his dying before she does? These questions haunted me for years after our brief encounter.

Getting off of work at 7 a.m. that morning, I started crying on the way to my car and was a complete blubbering mess by the time I plopped into the driver's seat. I let myself cry, but I also wanted to be home and go to bed to try and forget the night before because I had to do it all over again the next night. Driving out of the parking deck with tears still flowing, I drove past his father. He was leaning up against a car and crying with his face in his hands. That triggered me to start sobbing, almost in a primal way. *How can life be so cruel?*

After my short drive home, I made it inside as I continued to sob. I went to the kitchen cabinet, grabbed a pint-sized glass, filled it a third of the way with ice, and then opened the freezer to grab the vodka. Filling the rest of the glass with vodka as I was sobbing was a moment of desperation. I had never been this affected by a single patient, and I had never cried, especially like this. As I chugged the vodka in one gulp, I hoped I would pass out shortly afterward as I headed to bed.

Lying in bed, I wondered, *What did I just do?* That was a ridiculous amount of alcohol, especially to drink all at once, but I just needed to sleep and forget. I did get some sleep, but forgetting the night was another story.

Those of us who dedicate ourselves to caring for other people often get stuck, forgetting to care for ourselves. It is so easy to get lost in the machine:

- Checking boxes in the electronic health record
- Hitting critical times for medication delivery in an emergency
- Clocking in
- Clocking out
- Staff meetings
- More charting in the electronic health record
- Eating cafeteria food with minimal nutritional value
- Patient satisfaction scores
- Restocking rooms
- Doing CPR
- Handling social issues for a patient
- Worrying about your productivity numbers

The list is endless.

In a system focused on clinical and operational metrics, the emotional impact on those delivering the care is often an afterthought. This was my experience, at least. I loved the high-stress moments of resuscitation and critical decision-making, but in the end, they led me to be burned out, grouchy, and no longer "a joy to have in class," shall we say.

Battling a tough relationship with alcohol was a side effect. Binge drinking was my go-to. Blacking out was a regular occurrence so that I could escape from all of the emotion I was holding onto for other people. Life is a constant curveball, but I was making it even harder on myself without even knowing it.

Through a lot of deep inner work, I learned how to let go and let emotions flow through me instead of settling in my core. Psychedelic-assisted healing work has been part of the long path of coming into the truest version of myself. This teenager was a specific case that came to me while on a psychedelic journey, and I realized that I was still holding onto the grief that his family experienced. I was able to release those emotions and had a better understanding of myself and how to move forward on a daily basis. I finally started to feel free.

My journey with psychedelics saved me from drinking myself to death and freed me from the emotional weight I had been carrying from my years as a paramedic.It held up a mirror to show me areas that I needed to develop within myself, and allowed me to grieve more efficiently. The intentional and reverent use of psychedelic medicine has provided more healing for me than I ever thought possible. The relationship I've developed with the medicine is incredibly beautiful, and I'm forever grateful for the guides and mentors who have helped me along the way.

Working with psychedelics in this way is different from the image you may have in your head. Getting trippy at a show or on the couch with your friends is what many people may think of when they hear about psychedelics, but the psychedelic healing work that I'm discussing is sacred and intentional. There is a lot of preparation work that is necessary and helpful prior to your medicine experience. As you go into the space of your medicine journey, there should be thoughtful intention setting and care provided throughout the entire journey. One of the first intentions that I went on a journey with was to decrease my dependence on alcohol and work through any outstanding grief from the death of my dad. I was also open to whatever else the medicine wanted to show me, and it led to a transformative experience.

You should dedicate uninterrupted time before and after the medicine journey to process and absorb everything that you've been shown, and you should consider working with a psychedelic integration coach or therapist in the days and weeks after so that you achieve the lasting change that you desire. Doing this type of work isn't taking a handful of magic mushrooms in a social setting and being silly. It's a deep inward inward-focused and powerful approach to untangling parts of you that may be a bit stubborn to release.

Part of the work I do now is guiding others through their experience and relationship with psychedelic-assisted healing and repair work. No, I don't provide the medicine, but I do provide guidance and support before, during, and after a medicine experience so that the person taking the psychedelics feels supported in doing the work to get the benefits that they desire.

Preparation and integration are the keys to transformation when working with psychedelics. Approaching this work with a high degree of intention allows you to achieve the best results. Getting lasting results when working with psychedelics is a process. The work starts the second you become interested in working with a different approach compared to what you've traditionally tried. Part of what makes this work lead to long-term results is the opening of a critical period in your mind or the neuroplasticity that provides space for your brain to create new neural connections in the days and weeks after your medicine journey.

Psychedelic medicines create neuroplasticity, or learning flexibility, in your brain. That is, they open a window for your brain and mind to be pliable or more receptive to cementing new behaviors and learning new things like when you were a child. Depending on the medicine you work with, the window of neuroplasticity is different. Ketamine is a few days, psilocybin is about two weeks, and ibogaine is several months. The gift of neuro-plasticity is one of the best benefits of psychedelic medi-cine work, and making sure you have a plan to soak up all of the possibilities that come with this will help you maxi-mize your end results. Reaping the benefits of this work through executing a thoughtful integration plan will help you maximize the investment you've made in yourself by doing this meaningful work.

Integration work is the "so what?" of psychedelic medicine work. It's taking what the medicine showed you and making changes to your daily life to get the results that you desire. Reminding yourself on a daily basis in the weeks after your medicine journey about your *why* so that when moments of temptation to stray from your plan arise, you have the clarity to make a different choice and cement that change in your open mind. Integration is choosing yourself in a thoughtful way, every day. It is knowing that you're working to come out on the other side of something big, in the best way possible.

Developing an appreciation for the gravity of clarity that psychedelics can provide will serve you well as you step into this work. Getting clear on your intentions for working with the medicine, figuring out which questions you want to ask the medicine, and figuring out what kind of experience you hope to have are all great areas to explore prior to sitting with the medicine. The medicine will take you where you need to go, but providing some guidance is always helpful. Depending on the medicine you work with, the journey on it can be from an hour to a couple of days in length.

During and after the medicine journey, it is helpful to begin to digest everything that was brought up for you. Writing things down and talking with your coach, guide, or sitter is very helpful. The days and weeks after sitting with medicine are the most powerful. This is the time to give your mind, body, and soul the space to adopt lasting change through your window of neuroplasticity. In the weeks after sitting with medicine, people who work with a coach to intentionally bring what they've learned into their daily lives will have the best and most lasting results. Many people continue working with a coach or therapist for a while after their medicine experience to get the maximum benefit as they invest in themselves.

Psychedelics should be used with care, preparation, and intention. It is helpful to have a baseline level of stability within your nervous system, work with an experienced guide, have a support system in place, and be committed to the work. The first step in developing a relationship with psychedelic medicine work is to educate yourself. My website (scan the QR code in the front or back of this book or head over to www.garetfree.com) has a list of resources that can be a starting place. Read, listen, and watch as much as you can. Write your questions down. Consider what you're hoping to accomplish by doing this type of work. Then, seek out a guide that will serve as your advocate as you step through your psychedelic medicine work journey.

A psychedelic guide is someone who has an evolved relationship with psychedelic medicine work, has done extensive self-study work, and studied the work more formally. Your guide should work to ensure that you have a safe, meaningful, and integrated experience. They should push your edges, help you get clear on your intentions, facilitate a safe container, and encourage you as you integrate. Just as with any other type of healing modality, there's not a one-size-fits-all approach, so stay curious when seeking out a guide to work with. Trust your gut.

When it comes to selecting which medicine to work with, there is a lot to consider. Access, intention, level of work you're ready for, and cost all play a major role in deciding which medicine to work with. My website has a guide to psychedelic medicine work that can help you wrap your head around what is next for you when considering which medicine to research more in-depth.

An additional decision to make when starting with psychedelic medicine work is microdosing or macrodosing. It's important to note that not all medicines can or should be used for microdosing, so please ensure you're doing your research and working with a guide that you trust.

Microdosing is a great place to start if you're looking to ease into psychedelic medicine work more gently, build a strong foundation of stability in your nervous system (this allows for the deeper work to flow with more ease on a macrodose), and create space for intentional work to thrive. Medicines such as kanna, psilocybin, mescaline, LSD, and ketamine can all be considered for a microdosing protocol, but care should be taken.

Microdosing will not create any visuals or body sensations. It's helpful to keep a journal or log about how you feel throughout the day when microdosing. Writing this down every day will be helpful for you to pick up on the subtle changes that flow in as you progress with your microdosing work. You likely won't *feel* anything, but you should notice gradual improvement in your mood, focus, creativity, and nervous system regulation. As with all psychedelic medicine work, approach microdosing with intention, and bring along other practices such as movement, breathwork, and meditation to get the biggest benefit. If this is new for you, work with a guide.

Macrodosing, or big experiences, are typically reserved for when you are ready to make a big shift in life. Are you ready to get unstuck and figure out what is holding you back? It may be time for a macrodose. Going into this level of work requires a high degree of reverence for the medicine and the work. Your intentions should be clear, and you should be preparing on a daily basis for a couple of months prior to your experience with the medicine. Intention setting, nervous system regulation, cleaning up your diet, calming your mind, nurturing your body, and ensuring you have a solid support system in place prior to the medicine experience will help facilitate the most impactful experience possible.

During your journey, you should be with a guide or sitter who has intentionally created a space for your safety, is conscious of your needs for the entirety of the trip, can shift the vibe based on the energy in the room, and can provide care and support as you continue your integration path. Big medicine experiences will change your life in the way that you need them to, so step into this work with a lot of care. Be sure to have an integration plan that includes a coach with experience in psychedelic integration. This will help provide accountability as you move through the days of neuroplasticity and maximize the benefit of investing in yourself in this meaningful way.

As the theme of this book shows, psychedelics aren't a "magic pill." They are simply powerful tools that can help your imposter within relax and give your true self space to shine as you keep up with all the other tools that have been mentioned in this chapter already. This section on psychedelics is for educational purposes only and should not be considered medical advice.

Who Are You?

Knowing who you are and having a strong sense of your true self is what you're working to develop. I'd be willing to bet that your true self has had to shrink because of everything that has happened to and around you throughout your life.

It's a horrible feeling. Your imposter self works so hard to protect you from the outside world and all the potential or actual heaviness that comes along with life. In the process, your true self becomes diminished and loses the ability to steer the ship that is your life. Your imposter within thinks that it knows better, but in reality, it just needs to know that your true self is able to protect the previously injured parts of you.

Deciding how the narrative of your past plays into your daily life is up to you. Are you a child abuse survivor, or were you once abused as a child? You can replace child abuse with any traumatic event in your past. The way you talk about your past in your present day matters. Is your trauma or your past your entire identity or just a chapter in your story that is over now? Does your trauma determine how you show up today, or have you done the work to release the control that it has over you in the present moment?

That was a lot, so I invite you to take a deep breath.

I don't make these bold statements to diminish the experience of anyone's trauma. I've been there myself and have had plenty of trauma to work through during my healing and repair journey. One of the best lessons I learned was to give my emotions their time and place, but not control. The same can be said for trauma and your past. When you're truly ready to move forward in your life, you have to release the narrative that your past dictates how you show up today. Your past, trauma, and hardships are only fuel to keep your imposter self alive, well, and thriving.

My challenge to you as you work through the process of elevating your mindset is to shed the layers of your past and what happened to you. Allow them to flow out of your body, bit by bit. Release yourself from them. Let. Them. Go.

Yep, it's hard work. I've been there, and I continue to work on a daily basis to ensure that parts of my past don't creep back into the forefront of my reality. You will feel friction with your imposter self as you do the work to release yourself from the past, so don't let the crunchy moments at the beginning of this work deter you from pushing on. I promise, it's worth it.

As you're doing the work to shed your past, your trauma, and the control that your imposter self has over you, your true self will begin to see daylight. It may feel uneasy at first, given the many years of control that your imposter self has had over you, but when your true self has space, the magic is just beginning.

Keep on doing the work. You will discover that new things bring you joy and that misery no longer has quite the firm grip on you. You will have opportunities fall into your lap that you never would have imagined possible. Life will feel good for no reason at all. When someone asks you about yourself, thoughts about your past and all the horrible things you've been through will no longer be the first things to pop into your mind. Instead, you will be excited to talk about what lights you up in this moment.

Your Turn

This chapter provides a lot of suggestions for improving your mindset, your relationship with your imposter self, and the connection between your mind, body, and soul. It's up to you to do the work so your true self can feel empowered and you can realize lasting change.

When you're ready, I invite you to work on getting to the next level, two weeks at a time. Want to rework your mornings? Make a change and stick to it for two weeks. At the end of the two weeks, evaluate the impact that the change has had on your mornings. Is this something that you want to continue? Do you want to make adjustments, or do you want to let it go?

When making changes to how you show up for yourself on a daily basis, I've learned that there is something magical about doing it for at least ten days before deciding if you like it or hate it. Instead of focusing on instant gratification, focus on showing up on a consistent basis. Remember, there's no quick fix, no pill to take, and no one is coming to save you.

Consider using an organizer like the one below for thirty days to track your progress as you work to elevate your mindset.

Habit	Day of the month																													
	1	2	3	4	5	6	7	8	9	10	11	12	13	14	15	16	17	18	19	20	21	22	23	24	25	26	27	28	29	30

Summary of the Tools Discussed in This Chapter:

- Everything happens as it's supposed to.
- Your past made you who you are today.
- Thoughts are just thoughts, not reality.
  - Your imposter within will do everything in its power to prevent you from being vulnerable.
  - Actively managing your thoughts will go a long way toward helping you move past them.
  - Meditation, movement, and morning pages will help you proactively manage your thoughts.
  - Your thoughts will always be there, but you choose how to respond to them.
- Define your values.
- Fall in love with yourself.
- Have a good relationship with yourself.
- The way you communicate matters.
- Walking, running, or having some cardio in your routine is essential.
- Meditation for your mind.
- Morning Pages will change your life.
- Resistance and weight training have numerous health benefits.
- Massage and body scrubs are not just a luxury.
- Skin care, especially your face.
- Manicures and pedicures influence how you show up in the world.
- Nutrition—eat good (for you) food.
- Sleep will make or break you.

- Create instead of being an average consumer.
- Play is one of the first ways that we learned.
- Vulnerability will change your life.
- Honesty will serve you better than you expect.
- Get rid of clutter.
- Psychedelic-Assisted Healing.
- Who are you?

5

Build Your Confidence Empire

What are you waiting for? Tomorrow isn't guaranteed.

The first person with an opinion on why you do what you do, what you do, and how you do it is you, so set the standard high and be an overachiever when it comes to your goals. If you aren't satisfied with the result of your work, don't expect to be invited to the table by others. If there is even a sliver of doubt about the quality of your work deep down in the core of your being, the imposter who lives in you will have space to run free once you get critical feedback.

Constantly being a work in progress, seeking feedback from others proactively, and always knowing that you've done your best will show your imposter self that there is nothing to protect, just some tweaking to be better.

When you're ready for this phase of work as you change your relationship with your imposter within, get ready to be amazed by the outcome. There is nothing better than investing in yourself and then sitting with an enjoyable outcome.

Getting your shit together is a journey. Some of us figure it out at a young age, while some of us don't get it figured out until later in life. Timing doesn't matter; doing the work is the powerful piece. This work isn't about simply waking up on time in the mornings and showing up. It's about leaning into being the best version of yourself so that there isn't space for your imposter self to see the light of day. When you do your best in an intentional way, the space for self-doubt diminishes.

Over the years, I eventually got my shit together. There have been many times when I was more together than at other times, and it took a lot of trial and error to even out the ebbs and flows of life. My time at Advisory Board taught me many lessons, but one thing I learned was a grounded sense of confidence.

Leaving the bedside and stepping into the business side of healthcare outside of the hospital opened my eyes to an entirely different side of the business of healthcare. I was surrounded by brilliant minds who were focused on staying sharp, delivering exceptional service to their clients, and building up those around them. Coming from the "eat your young" mentality that was so prevalent in the early days of my career, I was amazed that there were so many smart and confident people who truly wanted to see their colleagues be successful.

As I settled in and started to become comfortable with my new professional reality, it was clear that my only option was to step up or step out. I decided to be a sponge, soaking up every bit of knowledge from the people around me while offering what I could in return. I was far from perfect, but this is where things really started to shift for me. I knew that I had a lot of work to do on myself if I wanted to enjoy the success that I was capable of achieving. I spent many late nights working away at home, learning new skills, preparing, rehearsing, and thinking so that I could show up like my colleagues.

The process in this chapter is what I've learned along the way and is very much a rinse-and-repeat model that can be used anytime you start a new job, are in a new relationship, or are given a new project to complete, from simple tasks such as washing the dishes to something more complex, like creating the next spaceship.

Speaking of the dishes, the dishwasher doesn't have to be full to run. Growing up, my parents required that the dishes be pre-washed and the dishwasher packed to the brim, as if the goal was to complete some intricate puzzle before turning the dishwasher on. I thought this was the only way to do it until I was at my friend Philip's house one evening and saw them putting messy plates (big chunks of food scraped off) in their dishwasher.

My mind was blown; there are no rules.

We fabricate these stories in our heads or take someone else's way of doing things as the only option instead of forming our own opinion and breaking free of the "this is how I've always done it" mindset. Building your Confidence Empire requires you to release yourself from your traditional ways of thinking and forge your unique path through life. Ultimately, it's up to you to figure out what works for you, but I'm sharing what I've learned in the hope that you don't have to endure as much trial and error as I lived through.

Define the Standard

Raise your hand if you've ever completed a task or project just to be told that you had done it incorrectly and it needed to be completely redone. Both of mine are raised.

One of the best lessons that I learned was to ask clarifying questions. When you are tasked with something, ask as many questions as possible. Then leave the door open by letting the assigner know that you may be back to ask additional questions once you have time to think and start your planning.

The thing is, when a request is made of you, it is highly probable that the person making the request has thought about ten times more instructions than they actually delivered to you. When you're defining the standard, you want to get into their mind. Seek to understand their point of view. Get into the nitty gritty. Create a dialogue with them so that you are getting your mind on as even a playing field as possible with theirs.

Taking instructions verbatim and completing the task or project without getting clarification often results in you doing extra work.

If you're drawing a blank at first, step away, do some thinking, and write out all the questions that come to mind. When you go back to ask clarifying questions, you will be spending everyone's time more efficiently while also getting what you need to be successful with what you've been tasked with.

Clarify the task first so that you are efficient when it comes time to deliver.

How Will You Be Measured?

During my time at Advisory Board, I was given a project that would be a key factor in determining my first promotion. It was a pretty big project, and I was nervous about meeting the expectations of the senior leaders on my team. Thankfully, I was able to get clarity on how I would be measured on the work I was doing. Knowing what would drive the critique of my work was a helpful guiding light. It gave me the space to think like the senior leaders, ask myself the questions that they might ask, and scrutinize my work like they might do as I developed the deliverable.

A part of me wanted to include this section with the "Defining the Standard" section, but I think it is important to separate "What does success look like?" from "How will success be measured?" As you're working through understanding what is expected, part of your initial interrogation should be used to get clarity on how you will be measured in the end. This will help you focus your efforts and mature your thinking on your process.

For bigger projects, get the answers in writing. This will help prevent a moving goal post and provide clear expectations in partnership with a clearly defined standard.

Questions that may be helpful when you're seeking clarity on how you will be measured:

- How will I be measured at the end? (I'm sorry to start so obviously)
- What does success look like for this project? How specific can I get?
- What is the deadline for completion?

- Is there an incentive to get this completed early?

Define Success for Yourself

This might be the most important step, especially when managing your imposter self. When I was working on that project at Advisory Board for my first promotion, I knew that I wanted to have a powerful deliverable and land strong with a solid presentation. Taking time to articulate this for myself kept me motivated throughout the project and gave me full control of the outcome. If I had approached this project with a laissez-faire attitude and the outcome hadn't led to me securing the promotion I was hoping for, my imposter self would have had space to find daylight and begun shouting the negative narrative that I didn't deserve the promotion.

If you want success, you have to begin by getting crisp on what that means for you. Chasing after someone else's idea of success will always lead to your disappointment. Before you invest too much time and energy in doing anything, consider spending a few minutes writing about what success looks like for you. Give yourself the power to define what your best work looks like and hold yourself accountable to that outcome. Sometimes, it will be simply showing up, but I challenge you to stretch yourself in defining what your best can be. Get specific. Don't shy away from setting goals for yourself that are achievable yet challenging.

Intentional activation of your internal motivation is the fuel for your success.

Develop Your Process

Having a process that aligns with the way you learn and work is so helpful, especially if that process allows you to move through it with intention. Your process will be different from those of other people. If you don't already have one, I invite you to do some writing or journaling about how you typically approach solving a problem or tackling a project. You may be surprised by what you come up with. If you're feeling stuck, here's a bit of my process to help you start thinking about your approach:

- Asking clarifying questions
- Getting clear on success
- Defining success for myself
- Doing research and information gathering
- Thinking about the solution and writing about ways to get there
- Seeking out additional opinions
- Asking for feedback along the way to ensure I'm headed in the right direction
- Constructing the deliverable
- Practicing the delivery
- Refining the deliverable and my delivery
- Delivering
- Getting feedback on success
- Debriefing on what I've learned

You'll see that much of my process for tackling a project or task is aligned with my "build your Confidence Empire" process, which helps keep my imposter self in check. I view every project or task as an opportunity to demonstrate to myself and others that I have my shit together, and there's no better way to do this than by following the formula that I know works.

Does this approach resonate with you? If not, what would you do differently?

How is your process different from mine?

If you haven't already, I encourage you to spend some time writing or journaling about your process and if there is anything specific that you'd like to lean into the next time you have a project or task to complete.

Execute Your Process

Have you heard the saying, "Actions speak louder than words"? I like to change that up a bit and say, "Results are better than ideas."

That mantra was one of the biggest drivers for me to write and get this book published. We all have millions of ideas that flow through our consciousness throughout our lifetime, but what do you do with those ideas? Ideas don't pay the bills. Ideas aren't successful.

Achieving results and getting to completion is the difference between people with great ideas and people with great success.

Sometimes, getting started can be the hardest part. Our minds or our imposter selves can take over our thoughts and paralyze us before we can begin tracking toward the results we need. This is why it is important to get your shit together and be clear on what your process is. Having clarity on what is expected and how you will be measured and defining success for yourself will help you keep your imposter self in check. This will provide the space for your creative self to shine through and get started on moving toward the finish line.

Do Your Research

Being curious will serve you well in all aspects of your life. Listen to understand instead of responding. Seek clarity so you can teach or articulate a concept back to someone. Learn something new. Evaluate different perspectives. Learn through someone else's lived experience. Get out of your comfort zone. Ask yourself, *"What am I missing?"* Find a source that you haven't used before. Accept that you don't have all the answers, regardless of who you think you are or what experience you have.

Information gathering through a critical-thinking lens is a very important skill and step to ensure that you are approaching the solution from the most grounded place possible. Validating sources, seeking out additional sources, and collecting conflicting viewpoints will help paint the most vivid picture possible.

Ask for Feedback Along the Way and Be Nimble

You will rarely be perfect the first time you attempt something. When entering into a new situation or being given a task or project, it will serve you well if you ask for feedback along the way instead of waiting until the end. I have learned this lesson the hard way a few times, getting through a fairly complicated project or presentation just to realize that I've completely missed the mark. This leads to duplicative energy and a full about-face. Asking for feedback along the way leads to small course corrections that will likely result in a better outcome.

A great lesson I learned a few years ago was to be nimble. When I got the chance to work with Jack Bonomo, he was the chief medical and quality officer at the largest health system in the State of New Jersey. He was incredibly wise, and even though I was the consultant doing work for him, he taught me many great lessons, like being nimble.

When you're working through something, whether it be making a decision, forging a new relationship, navigating a social situation, completing a project, or delivering a presentation, it can be helpful to seek feedback from your audience, peers, or superior to ensure that what you're putting out there is landing in the way that you believe that it should. If it's not, you have an immense opportunity to make some adjustments so that you get to a satisfactory endpoint more efficiently.

A nimble mindset provides the space to adjust, rework, rethink, or convey your message in a different way so that you bring your audience along with you on a productive journey instead of hoping that they understand the way you think.

Ways to seek out feedback:

- "Thank you for trusting me with completing this work. Can I schedule time with you in a week to review my progress and get feedback on the direction I'm going?"
- "I've been speaking for a few minutes, and I'm curious if this all is landing and I'm heading in a direction that makes sense for the group. What questions do you have, or what else would you like me to cover?"
- "We've been working together for a little over two months now. Can you share your experience working with me? What can I do better?"

- "These first few dates with you have been very enjoyable for me. How are you feeling about our dynamic?"
- "Our conversation has been very engaging for me so far. How do you feel about what we've discussed?"
- "Thank you for taking some time to review what I've been working on. Here's what I've completed so far, but I'm feeling stuck in this one area. Can you review what I've completed so far and provide some guidance on how I might get this completed?"
- "I'm feeling really good about this project so far. What am I missing from your perspective?"
- "This data seems to be showing one thing, but I was expecting something else. Do you have any guidance on a different way to look at this problem?"
- "Here's what I plan to cover today during our scheduled time. Does anyone have anything else that they would like to add to the agenda?"

It can be so easy to go into our own inner world and deliver on our own agenda. Your imposter within can make it easy to allow fear to take over by telling you that other people don't matter and that you have all the answers. In reality, the collective brainpower of those around you will most often lead to a more positive and productive outcome.

Constructing the Deliverable

This step can often be the most difficult. It's where the rubber meets the road, and you have to produce. It's not about the idea; it's about the action. Ideas are great, but action is where the magic lies.

Successful people deliver results on their ideas.

Those who never do anything with their ideas might as well have never had the idea to begin with.

Building the presentation, writing the book, going on that first date, or building that new relationship takes intentional work—blood, sweat, and tears, as some people say. It can be very easy for this to seem overwhelming, but you will serve yourself well if you approach everything with intention.

Your imposter within thrives on making the end result seem impossible. Not being able to see the forest for the trees, not being able to get started, not knowing where to start, feeling nervous about saying "hello," being a nervous wreck before taking the stage, or feeling like you're going to do or say the wrong thing are all examples of the imposter within having too much space.

My journey to writing this book is a prime example of me having to regularly keep my imposter within at bay. This book started with an idea, but then I didn't know what to do next. I wrote an outline that didn't feel right, I felt forced to start writing, and I questioned if this was even worth my time. I navigated a range of emotions: uncertainty, self-doubt, fear, and anxiety about ever being able to complete this project. It was a very familiar journey, one that I've had in my personal and professional lives for many years.

However, once I surrendered to the process of writing this book in an intentional way, the words started to flow. Writing for this book became something that I looked forward to every day, and I had it finished in a much shorter timeline than I ever thought possible.

This is why getting your shit together is so critical to taking the power back from your imposter within. Doing the work on a daily basis to build the necessary confidence so that you can execute is the required practice for your success.

When working through this step, I invite you to think about the process of eating an elephant. What seems like a massive undertaking can only be achieved one way—one bite at a time. You're not going to be successful if you try to get the entire elephant eaten at once, but if you take your time in an intentional way, enjoy the process, and trust yourself along the way, the elephant will be gobbled up sooner than you expected.

When you're crafting your deliverable, think about the most efficient way for you to get it done.

Projects:

- Plan what you want to create. Think about dedicating a notebook or journal to creating. Write about what is needed. Write about how you want to solve the problem. Draft and re-draft an outline. Then refer back to what you've written in your notebook when it's time to build. This process helps you get your thoughts on a physical landing space and prevent your imposter within from controlling your actions when it's time to create.

- Dedicate small amounts of time to focus intensely on what you're creating. Your imposter within will want you to check your email or phone notifications or have the TV on in the background. I invite you to clear all distractions for a predetermined time and focus solely on creating. Take a small break and then get back to another focus block if that's what you have scheduled. For this book, I would write for thirty-three minutes and thirty-three seconds at a time. In between, I'd take a break to stretch, get some water, check my phone, or go for a walk. Doing this gave my mind the space to be squarely focused on getting words on paper and prevented the thoughts of my imposter within from running free.

- When planning your timeline to complete your project, ensure that there is time for your deliverable to sit and rest. Revisit it after a day or two to review and edit. This may result in small tweaks, no changes, or a complete overhaul. Do this as many times as necessary until you feel settled with what you've created. This process will prevent your imposter within from having an opinion when you're crossing the finish line.

- As you're nearing the end, polish your work. After the content or meat of the project is settled, spend time looking at the details. Tidying up all the minor details before declaring completion will prevent your imposter within from sneaking in after you expected to be finished. This is where you

126

check things like spelling, grammar, and consistency with font size, sand the rough edges, tighten all the screws, glue down the corners, and make sure that—as some people say—all of your i's are dotted and your t's are crossed.

Relationships:

- When you're looking to improve your relationships, I invite you to first get clear on who you are. What defines you? What are your values? What is your guiding light? How have you grown over the years? What areas do you still want to focus your growth on? This is where a coach or therapist can be helpful. Doing the work on yourself first will pay so many dividends when you're looking to show up as your true and best self in a relationship with someone, something, or someplace.
- After you've invested in yourself, do some introspection on what types of relationships you're looking to invite into your life. Are you looking for a partner? Are you ready to evolve the relationship with your current partner? Are you ready for more supportive friendships? Does the relationship with your parents need some love and care? Are you looking to change your relationships with alcohol or other substances? Are you looking to find a healthier balance with work? Are you looking to find purpose in your life outside of the bar scene? Your imposter within will tug on you to stay anchored to people, places, and things that do

not serve your true self. Your imposter within is likely on the low end of the vibe scale and will pull you in that direction constantly. When it's time for you to evolve past this low-vibe state, your relationships will have to evolve if you desire sustainable change, so get clear on the direction that you desire to head toward.

- Once you're clear on the direction that you want to head, start placing yourself in situations that align with your desired types of relationships. If you're ready to move from drinking every weekend to once a month, then consciously choose to do so. If you're ready for a partner, begin dating with intention. If you're ready for improved friendships, lean into vulnerability. If you're ready to improve your relationship with your parents, focus on boundaries and improved communication. These are all interchangeable examples. Evolving your relationships is tough work, but you can get there with a bit of focus and intention.

- Be ready for a period of loneliness. When you're growing and leaving your old ways behind, your imposter within will get lonely. The lifting of the weight of your old ways will be challenging to navigate. Your true self will have to regularly show up as the leader of your happiness. It's okay to spend time alone during this time as you give your imposter within time to be released from the relationships that don't serve your true self and long-term goals.

- Put yourself in uncomfortable and new situations. Your imposter within will push you to return to your comfort zone, but if you truly want to release it, you have to do something different. Find a new job, set boundaries, lean into your artist self, try a new hobby for ninety days, or start exercising regularly, meditating, doing yoga a couple times a week, or creating instead of consuming. Focus on progress instead of perfection because progress *is* perfection.

Presentations:

- Some people are natural presenters. They command attention with ease while speaking about any subject. That's not the case for everyone, though. For many people, the imposter within can come out screaming with fervent energy when it's time to present. That's why it's so important to be prepared when it comes to what you will deliver, how to navigate unexpected responses from the audience, and how to manage uncomfortable moments.
- If presenting is new to you, I highly recommend reading *The Exceptional Presenter* by Timothy J. Koegel. This book (along with some in-person classes and a lot of practice) helped shape how I present to a room full of people.
- Start by planning what you will deliver. Think about telling a story instead of delivering content. Imagine being in the audience, and what would keep you engaged. Consider what will distract your audience and how to manage through that. How do you craft a presentation

that will give the audience enough information to ask questions and want to know more?

- As much as I hate to admit it, our high school English teachers were right: an outline helps. Wrapping your head around the flow of a presentation (or the story that you will be telling) through an outline will help you be more efficient later when you're filling in the details. Your imposter within will fight you on this because it seems like unnecessary work that won't add value to the final product. However, this is an excellent opportunity for your true self to take charge and surrender to the process.

- Once your outline is complete, consider asking for feedback. Make sure you're headed in the right direction and prevent your imposter within from having space later on when you might have a lot of reworking to do if you don't get that feedback.

- When you're in a good spot, fill in the gaps. What needs to be added to your outline so that a more complete story can be told during your presentation? What details can be left out? What can you share that will spark questions throughout your presentation or toward the end? At which moments do you engage the audience to keep their attention? If you're giving a long presentation, do you need to give the audience a break at some point?

- Develop your notes, slide deck, or other visual aids. Remembering that people learn differently (audio, visual, tactile, etc.) and incorporating all of those ways into your presentation will help set you up for success. Many years ago, I developed and taught a class on EKG interpretation for firefighters and paramedics. Toward the end of the class, I split everyone into small groups and spread shaving cream over the tables. The groups then had to draw out the visuals (QRS complex for my healthcare friends) for all the different cardiac conditions. It was a fascinating exercise to watch the groups work together to implement what they had learned and draw it out—the shaving cream added a layer of play. It's one thing to consume, but it's a very different experience to create.

- Just as you would with projects, polish your presentation and the deliverable. When working through a slide deck, I like to approach the polishing in a methodical way, starting with the title of each slide and then moving to the fonts for all slides, then the white space, then the borders, then the footnotes, etc. Being intentional and methodical will help you move more quickly and get to the end without feeling totally overwhelmed.

Navigating a social situation:

- As an extroverted introvert, finding myself in new social situations can be daunting. My imposter within loves to tell me that I don't belong, sending an immense wave of self-doubt to wash over me.
- Choosing where and how I show up in social situations has become super important to

preventing my imposter within from taking over when I show up in a social situation. Be clear on your intention for why you're going somewhere or participating in some activity prior to getting there. Put care and intention into what you wear so that you look smart. Arrive with a sober mind so that you are able to be fully present as you settle into the space and engage with other people in an intentional way.

- Chill out with the alcohol. Don't show up hungover and don't show up with a pregame buzz. If you're someone who can have one or two drinks, then great! Do your thing. For many people, however, one drink can lead to many. Once you get to a certain point with the alcohol, the ability to communicate in an intentional way starts to get a bit blurry. Space starts to open up for miscommunication and regrettable conversations, and actions.

- If you're going into a one-on-one situation, especially for the first time, have a few meaningful questions ready to ask the other person. Your imposter within will want to keep you nervous and feeling like you don't know what to say, but if you are prepared, it will make it much easier for your nerves to settle and for you to engage in meaningful conversation.

Practice Your Delivery

Don't skip this step. For many years growing up, I was great at winging it. I played oboe and alto sax in band and was just good enough that I didn't have to practice much at home to get by at school. However, this didn't play out well in my adult life. Adulting presents problems and situations that are much more complicated to navigate, and there are far more people competing for the space that you've been given. You need to be pretty damn good at what you do to be seen and to be successful.

This is where practicing comes in. Regardless of what you're facing, a project, presentation, relationship, or new social situation, practice your delivery. Your imposter within will tell you that practicing is silly and a waste of time, but give your true self the necessary agency to take charge and practice.

The shower is a great place to practice for a presentation, an upcoming conversation, or how you will navigate a new social situation. Doing a dress rehearsal with yourself will help to provide the space to think through the possible scenarios that may arise on the day in question. Spend time talking out loud to yourself about how things may go, the questions you may receive, and what you'll do if something goes awry.

Preparation through repetition will always serve you well. The more you practice, the better you'll perform. Having note cards, PowerPoint slides, or a script memorized may be helpful for some, but I encourage you to be so comfortable with your material that when you show up, the majority of your performance flows from you naturally.

Refine Your Approach

Many times, less is more. Your imposter within may tell you all kinds of stories to get you worked up and nervous prior to your big moment, but that may be an opportunity to get crisper or refine your approach. As you start to work on something, it should evolve and end up in a different state than how it started.

Most adults have a very short attention span, so consider exactly how much someone can absorb when you're getting to the end of developing your deliverable. For a work deliverable, use no more than ten slides for an hour-long presentation. For a new social situation, focus on three or so meaningful topics of conversation. For a project, isolate one meaningful outcome that can be broken into three subtopics. For your relationship with your partner, check in weekly on your relationship, where both of you can seek clarity and ask about anything on your minds. This isn't an exhaustive list, but hopefully, it gives you a framework for what you're looking to accomplish with your assignment, deliverable, or relationship.

Deliver on Your Assignment

It's not easy to take a leap of faith and try something new or better yourself, but if you've done the work to be prepared to the best of what you have available to you, then now is your time to shine. When the time arrives for you to execute, pause. Close your eyes. Take a few slow, intentional, deep breaths. Personally, I like to breathe in for four seconds, hold my breath for seven seconds, and then exhale for eight seconds. This activates your vagus nerve, which will slow your heart rate down and help you relax. Remind yourself of all the preparation work you've completed. Allow the goodness that you've invested in to settle into your body.

Go into the moment with no expectations—that is, don't get married to an outcome. Stand up straight, with your shoulders back, and feel a smile wash over your face. It is your time to shine.

I could ramble on about tips and tricks for delivering more effectively, but that's probably better left for another time. It all comes down to preparation. I've learned that ninety percent of successfully releasing your imposter self from the need to create a negative narrative in your mind comes from preparation work, and ten percent comes from how you deliver on that preparation.

Intentional investment from the start will result in exceptional delivery.

Debrief on What You Have Learned

Congratulations! You've made it through your project, improved a relationship, delivered your presentation, or navigated a new social situation. I hope that you feel proud of yourself and that you are starting to see the confidence that comes from achieving your goals. Sit back for a minute and enjoy the feeling of being proud of yourself for getting to this point.

It would be amazing if I could say that the work is over, but it's really just getting started. One of the biggest pieces of building your Confidence Empire is taking a step back and inventorying everything you've learned through this process. Take notice of your success through this process. Identify what could have been done better. Make a list of areas or edges that need additional exploration. Feel good about your progress and get ready to tackle your next adventure.

Handling your imposter within is an ongoing process of growth. If I've learned anything, it's that you have to keep growing and improving your character if you want to keep your inner imposter in check. The imposter within thrives when there is a window of stale energy that opens for them to shine through. Continuous growth by regularly upscaling your vibe will keep your energy fresh and your imposter within in its place, tucked away behind your true self.

During this phase of getting your shit together, it can be helpful to write about this experience. Sit down with your journal and set a timer for thirty-three minutes and thirty-three seconds (if you're like me and like repetitive numbers) or, if twenty minutes sounds more palatable, start with that. Start with the writing prompt: *"What has _____ taught me?"* Fill in the blank with the project, relationship, presentation, or social situation that you've been working through.

Spend the remainder of the time dedicating space to getting super specific about what you've learned about your imposter within and your true self. Explore where that learning may have come from. Some specific topics to consider include:

- Take what you've learned and ask yourself, what's under it?
- What do you need to do to crystallize this learning so that it stays with you?
- Is there something that needs to change in your everyday life based on this experience?
- How can you move through this process more fluidly and crisply in the future?

- Knowing what you know now, what will you do differently in similar situations?
- Who do you need to debrief with?
- What vulnerable conversations need to be had?
- What self-education should you explore to be better?
- When you run into obstacles in the future, how will you react based on this experience?

Wrapping It Up

Take a deep breath. Hold it at the top for a second. Take in one last sip of air so that this is the deepest breath you've taken all day.

Now release it and let it go.

This chapter is a long one because it requires work. Building your Confidence Empire is a process, and it's not something that happens overnight. Some people figure it out when they're very young; other people don't figure it out until later in life.

It doesn't matter *when* you start the work of building your Confidence Empire.

What matters is your *why,* that you are focused on getting started, and that you are regularly dedicating time to figuring this all out. Your imposter self grew inside you over a long period of time, so it is going to take some time to untangle it from your everyday life.

I know for sure (thank you, Oprah, for this powerful phrase) that if you do the work, you will be successful. Your true self's job is to focus on the progress needed to regain the energy that the imposter within sucked away. I hope that this chapter can be a guide to support your growth and help you find a better relationship with your imposter self.

Confidence is sexy, but it takes work. Imagine getting started now and think of all the benefits you can realize in a very short period of time. If you truly want to change the relationship with your imposter self, building a solid Confidence Empire will serve you for the rest of your life. You will be unstoppable.

6

Exploration in Your Confidence Empire

A strong daily dose of humility will take you a long way. It's not good enough to build a Confidence Empire; you need to understand what that means for how you show up in a grounded way every day. If you thought the work was over after the last chapter, it's not. We are here to keep going, to continue to push the envelope of what is possible, and to show our imposter selves that our true selves are set to thrive.

This chapter contains short essays on mindset shifts that make a big difference for me and my clients. As you absorb them, I encourage you to take some time to think about how each topic can show up in your daily life. Consider if this is something that you have the capacity to implement today or if you want to come back to it in the future.

Finding Alignment With Your Life

Understanding alignment didn't happen for me until I finally experienced it. I didn't even know it was a thing. I was wandering through life with minimal direction, going through the motions, and waiting for happiness to fall into my lap. It wasn't until I defined my values, started making decisions based on those values, and chose to invest in myself every day that alignment and happiness started to find me. Society has one way of teaching us how to live life, but why do we think we have to subscribe to that?

Alignment in life is when your body, mind, and soul all feel settled and happy with the current moment and the direction you're headed. It means making decisions for your true self instead of your imposter self and feeling empowered to take the path that feels right for you, not because someone else wants you to go that direction. Alignment is moving through *your* life with minimal friction.

Chasing more money and more stuff was the rat race I found myself in for many years. I didn't know any better, but as I exceeded my salary goals time and time again while working for someone else, I was wound up, miserable, and, at times, suicidal. My bank account was sitting pretty, but my emotional tank had a rusted-out bottom. My physical self wasn't much better, either.

One fall afternoon, I was sitting in the exam room of a cardiologist's office because my heart palpitations were so frequent that I had become worried about them. I asked myself, *"How the fuck did I get here?"* Despite my age and risk factors being low for anything serious to be of concern, I still wanted peace of mind through an echocardiogram and wearing a heart monitor for a week. The cardiologist was a little entertained by me, I think, but I needed reassurance that I wasn't going to drop dead the next day.

Everything checked out fine, but it was a wake-up call for me to begin resetting my priorities. Working more than sixty hours a week was no longer an option if I couldn't exercise daily. Alcohol was no longer a weekly occurrence, maybe once a month. Yoga needed to become more regular again. Meditation had to happen every day. Taking a week off of work every quarter was a requirement. My body was begging to be loved, so I listened.

Once I became more intentional with how I showed up for myself, I realized that balance and alignment were necessary if I wanted to live with any longevity and quality. I was ready to leave my last full-time job when I got the blessing of being laid off. It was just what I needed to reset and recover from the grueling pace that I had been living for so long.

As I settled into what was next for me professionally, I decided to build my own business. While that was a big challenge, I had the space to rediscover and crack open my creative self while building something that made sense for me. I was my own boss, and it felt good knowing that I was completely responsible for determining my outcome.

Then the craziest thing happened. I started writing, and the idea for this book fell into my lap. It was a surreal experience—about two months later, I was already halfway through with the first draft of this book, an amazing feat for someone who had HATED writing while in school.

However, when I look back, I realize that everything happened just as it was supposed to. I was at the stage of my journey with healing and repairing my relationship with my imposter self where I was ready to share what I had learned with other people. Combine that with my freshly cracked-open creative self, and it was a recipe for magic.

The opportunity to create a book that will last much longer than I ever will felt so good. The opportunity to build a coaching practice to help people move the needle in their own lives in a meaningful way also felt amazing. Finding what lights me up and committing to executing on it was the alignment that I needed. I felt confident that all the investments I'd made in myself and my career were paying off. Feeling in alignment meant that I knew that I was right where I was supposed to be. Who knows what will happen after this book is published, but for now, it feels amazing to be doing work every day that aligns with nourishing my mind, body, and soul in an intentional way.

Seek Out Opposing Viewpoints

You will never have all the answers. If you're the smartest person in the room, you need to find a different room. Collective intelligence will win every time compared to perceived individual brilliance.

Throughout my life, I've always chosen to surround myself with people who don't look or think like me or who came from different backgrounds than I did. It's served me well, as they have often pointed out something critical I was missing or showed me a more efficient way to do something.

If you don't have good people in your corner who challenge the way you think, you're making a huge mistake. You don't always have to agree with them, but you need to be challenged. Staying in your same lane of comfortable thinking and feeling like you have all the answers necessary for a fulfilling life is a fast-track ticket to misery. You need viewpoints from people who don't look like you, have different lifestyles from you, and come from different socioeconomic backgrounds to push your edges.

The power of diversified points of view lies in being able to expose your blind spots that you didn't even realize were there. Your imposter self may tell you that you have to have all the answers, or people will think you are a fraud and don't know what you're doing, but it is just trying to protect you from something that hasn't happened yet, a made-up scenario.

To show your imposter self that it is safe to release control of having all the answers, try having conversations or leading meetings where you just listen. Ask people what they think with no agenda behind it, no expectation, and no response other than gratitude for them sharing their perspective. Not everything has to be a debate.

The ultimate goal when seeking out opposing viewpoints is to find the best solution. Proactively seeking out what others think will give you extra data to chew on as you process through your decision-making process. It will help ground you in realities other than your own, and you will be able to have a bigger impact, given that you got out of your own way.

Challenge the Status Quo

"That's the way we've always done it."

Well, who gives a shit? Sometimes, you need to throw the baby out with the bathwater and start over. Other times, you need to rethink why you're throwing the bathwater out in the first place.

I've never been one to accept that the way we've done things historically should naturally be adopted by everyone. Being curious about the *why* behind the what has led me to some interesting places, including writing this book. Do you want to improve your relationship with your imposter self? Once you have a solid foundation, start by meaningfully and intentionally challenging the status quo in your everyday life. Do you clean your bathroom once a month? How about changing that to once a week? A shiny, clean sink does wonders for the soul.

Success comes to those who are willing to take a chance and do something differently. You can't stay in the same routine, doing the same thing, day after day, and expect greatness to fall in your lap. Maybe that works for a select few, but to carve your own path, you have to move in a different way.

Is a process not crisp at work? Take on the work of dissecting it and rebuilding it from the ground up. Use a couple of these projects to build the case for a promotion.

Is there friction in one of your relationships? Take a strong look in the mirror and make sure you're showing up as someone you'd want to be in a relationship with.

Having a hard time finding a job? Make sure you're interviewing like someone you (or better yet, the interviewer) would hire.

Have crippling anxiety? Work with a coach, therapist, healer, trainer, nutritionist, holistic practitioner, somatic practitioner, art therapist, hypnotherapist, psychedelic guide, or acupuncturist until you get to know and understand what the underlying cause is.

Staying stuck in your life is an acceptable choice if you're truly at peace with how your life flows every day. However, if feeling stuck isn't the pattern that you want to repeat every day, ask yourself what needs to be challenged and done differently. Something as simple as a small adjustment to your morning routine or adding a walk in the afternoon can do wonders for shaking loose the sludge that may be holding you back.

As you continue working through small adjustments in your life, a time will naturally flow in that will allow for larger shifts to occur. If you want to find progress and change in your life, start with small challenges to prepare yourself for the big shifts that are yet to come.

Become Comfortable With Being Uncomfortable

After being at Advisory Board for a couple of years, I realized that I had developed a new skill: being comfortable with being uncomfortable. Sitting in silence in tense moments, taking a pause after someone said something questionable, and asking the awkward questions helped me understand that people need time to think and sit with something challenging. Going from the bedside to the boardroom was no easy transition, but realizing that, sometimes, the smartest person in the room is the quietest helped me achieve my goals.

You don't always have to have the answer, but creating the space for it to be cultivated is where your power lies. In moments of tension, taking a pause to allow people to think and mentally digest the conversation will serve you well. Your imposter self may start with a conversation in your head based on the fear of being found out as a fraud, telling you that you need to have the answer to keep the conversation moving, but what if you just stayed quiet and gave the conversation time to breathe? What if you waited until the tension in the room was obviously palpable? You might find that just when you think no one can take it anymore, someone suddenly introduces a powerful question or the next great idea to move the conversation forward.

Sitting in discomfort takes practice. I remember walking out of meetings feeling so grateful that I had on an undershirt because I was drenched with sweat from forcing myself to stay quiet, as the meeting had been full of awkward silences and uncomfortable moments. However, as I honed this skill, I saw that my results improved.

Take Accountability for Your Outcome

No one is coming to save you, so it's up to you to figure your life out. Even if you do all the work described in this book, it will still be up to you to take control of your destiny. Look at how many lottery winners blow all the money they receive and end up in the same position they were in prior to winning. How many trust fund kids have it all figured out and are happy humans? Regardless of the "luck" that lands (or doesn't) in your lap, it is your responsibility to chart the path that aligns with your goals and dreams. There's no magic spell. You have to take accountability and do the work.

This really hit home for me after my mom died. With both of my parents now gone, it was a bit of a wake-up call that I was responsible for my destiny. There was no fallback. While I've always felt fairly independent, I realized that there was still a small narrative in the back of my head telling me that any risk I took would be okay since I still had Mom and Dad to fall back on, just in case something didn't work out. Without the safety net they provided, the choice I made was to do the work, chart my own path, and create the best life possible for my true self to thrive.

Quit Apologizing Unless You've Intentionally Done Something Wrong

We are all human, and we're going to make the wrong move many times in our lives. However, if you're constantly apologizing for your actions, you're training your mind to think that you're always wrong. Consider the intention behind your actions prior to apologizing. Bring daylight to your intentions and acknowledge how your actions made someone else feel. Accept responsibility for learning from your behavior and then make changes in how you show up. Be genuine.

Apologizing all the time gives your necessary apologies less weight. If an apology is truly warranted, there should be a conversation in detail where you are creating space for the other person or people who were affected to share the impact of your choices on them. You should come to the table with more than "I'm sorry." There should be more meat on those bones. Saying, "I'm sorry that my poor decision caused you to feel mistreated, and in the future, I'm going to take a pause and think prior to speaking about you in a public setting without you being there," goes much further. It shows your commitment to improving yourself.

Quit Giving Advice Unless Someone Asks for It

Sometimes, we just want to be heard.

That's a lesson I've had to learn time and time again. Like most of us, I've always been very opinionated, and I like having done the research to back up my stance. When I share something, I want it to make sense and leave an impact. However, it's not always about me and what I want. I'm a great listener and had to learn that I don't always need to insert my opinion into a conversation.

When someone tells you their problems, ask them if they want you to listen, give advice, or respond in another way. I've had to learn this lesson time and time again. When you're supporting a friend, partner, coworker, or direct report, asking them what they need instead of giving them what you think they need will go a long way toward deepening your bond with them and showing them that you support them as a fully autonomous person.

While I love giving my opinion, learning that I only need to share it when it is welcome has helped me overcome numerous relationship issues.

Grace

We all deserve to receive and give equal amounts of grace: to those we love, to strangers, to animals, to the earth. As mentioned previously, we are all imperfect humans, and I've yet to meet anyone who is a mind reader. You never know what obstacle someone else is navigating in the moment, but you can extend them a bit of grace instead of cultivating a ball of anger inside of yourself. Accept that the world doesn't revolve around you, and there are people out there having a harder time than what you may be experiencing.

As I was doing the work to heal and repair myself, I learned to give my parents grace. In exploring concepts like the patriarchy (shout-out to bell hooks and *The Will to Change*) and how the interpretation of the Bible has evolved over time, and reflecting on how I was a stubborn kid, I realized that my parents were so deserving of grace. While my childhood may not have been perfect through the lens that I viewed it with, I also hadn't been a perfect child. My parents did the best they could with what they had access to, and that's a lot more than what many kids get. Instead of holding on to needless anger, I learned to release it in the form of grace.

The next time someone, especially someone you don't know, sparks anger or frustration in you, say out loud, "They're doing the best they can," instead of whatever you might traditionally say. This practice will take some repetition for you to see the benefit, but you will soon notice that you have a very different visceral response when someone cuts you off in traffic, leaves the toilet seat up, doesn't empty the coffee grounds from the coffee pot, or is five minutes late to the meeting they scheduled.

Be known as the person who isn't fazed by the actions of others. Don't be known as the person who can't seem to ever get anything done because everyone else's actions are driving their poor behavior.

No Is a Complete Sentence

You don't always have to explain yourself. If you don't want to do something or aren't interested, a simple "no" will often suffice. Take inventory of the times in your life when you spent too much time and energy justifying why you didn't want to do something. It might have been due to your imposter self showing up as self-doubt. Are you providing a justification to make your imposter self feel better? Your reasoning can often make your imposter self feel more empowered. Are you giving out an unnecessary explanation because you think someone else's feelings will be hurt? Other people are responsible for managing their own feelings.

Quit the mental gymnastics that are necessary as you mollify other people's potential response to your "no."

There are times when a simple "no" will not cut it, but I'd push you to consider allowing whoever you're engaging with to ask for the explanation instead of feeling like you're required to always provide it. For decisions in which you have time to think about your response, consider having a reason prepared if one is needed. For in-the-moment decisions, ask if you can have time to prepare your response if it is required. Even if you only take a few deep breaths to give your brain time to relax and process, it can help you come to your response with clarity instead of rambling.

Cultivate an Abundance Mindset

It's too easy to always focus on everything that's wrong in your life. I'm guilty of doing this on a regular basis. In fact, while working on this chapter, I've had to pull myself out of a funk because the fear of the unknown, as I get close to finishing and publishing this book, has weighed heavily on me over the last couple of days.

However, if you stay focused on the negative aspects of life, it becomes so much easier to identify and resonate with the negative. You will continue down the apathy spiral when you give your mind the runway to chase after negative thoughts. But! Just as with a negative spiral, if you work on cultivating an abundant mindset, it will be easier to focus on all the positive aspects of your life.

It may not be easy to get started, but if you do all the other steps in this book to better manage your relationship with your imposter self, you will already be setting the stage for your abundant mindset to flourish. Beginning the day by recognizing that you woke up and that you're breathing is the start of building your abundant mindset. From there, allow the challenges of the day to be moments in time instead of defining milestones.

Continue to focus on and resonate with what goes right. Appreciate the impact of every step that you take, regardless of how small it is. Celebrate the small successes so that you're creating space for the big wins. Focus on progress and be happy when something small comes together. Acknowledge that making it through the day was a success, and instead of always debriefing on everything that went wrong, make sure that you're creating space to sit with what went right.

Abundance isn't about money. It's about fulfillment. It's about having the capacity to share. It's about choosing to create space for the positive. It's about releasing the bad and the evil. It's about having agency over and choosing to control your mental playground. It plays well into gratitude.

Gratitude

If you don't already start every day with gratitude, I challenge you to do so today. Leading life through the lens of gratitude will pay significant dividends, especially during the hard times. Gratitude is a special concept that opens many doors for you once you begin to lead your life with it on full display. Your imposter within doesn't appreciate gratitude because of the negative impact it has on its ego. Your imposter self wants to hold you back, while gratitude helps to propel you forward. Being grateful for everything in life, from the small things to the bigger life events, will help you shift your mindset in a powerful way.

Practicing gratitude is a daily ritual for me. I start with my morning pages, writing about five things that I'm grateful for, and I try not to repeat anything very often. Many days, I'll also sit with whatever I'm grateful for and notice how my body feels and include that observation in my morning pages. This is incredibly helpful for the mind-body connection that is vital for your healing and repair work.

So, what are you grateful for? No matter how big or small, take a moment and consider a few things that you're truly grateful for from the last twenty-four hours. If you have a journal or notebook, spend some time writing about them. When you're done—and for the rest of the day—pay attention to how you feel.

As you progress in your gratitude practice, notice moments of gratitude throughout your day and make a mental note of them. When you have a challenging situation, say an argument with your partner or family member, be grateful for what you learned as you worked through the disagreement instead of holding on to negative emotions. This mindset shift will help you sustain an improved relationship with your imposter self as you navigate the work to give your true self space to shine.

Your Turn

There is a lot to digest in this chapter, and I encourage you to take each concept and investigate it further when it makes sense for you. For this moment, which mindset shift really resonated with you? Spend some time writing about it and why it seems to resonate with you the most. Then I invite you to start practicing it today, even in the smallest form. Start small and allow momentum to bring it into your life more fully.

Summary of the Tools in This Chapter:

- Finding alignment with your life
- Seek out opposing viewpoints
- Challenge the status quo
- Become comfortable with being uncomfortable
- Take accountability for your outcome
- Quit apologizing unless you've intentionally done something wrong
- Quit giving advice unless someone asks for it
- Grace
- No is a complete sentence
- Cultivate an abundance mindset
- Gratitude

7

Sharing Your Confidence Empire

Confident people share their success. They don't keep things to themselves. As you regularly invest in yourself and conquer your relationship with your imposter self, your newfound confidence will likely create a desire within your soul to share the success you've stepped into. Giving generously not only feels good, but it also organically builds community. The world needs more confident people who are focused on building up those around them while also doing the work on themselves.

As you track toward thriving in the joyful life you've created for yourself, you will want to be around people of a similar vibe, people who are investing in themselves on a regular basis so that they, too, can get the most out of the precious life they've been given.

Sharing your Confidence Empire comes in all shapes and sizes. Just as with the dishwasher example, there are no rules. You can:

- Change the conversations you have with friends and family.
- Show up as a more heart-centered leader at work.
- Volunteer more regularly.
- Mentor someone in a different phase of life.
- Start your own company.
- Write a book.
- Share differently on social media.
- Re-think your career path.
- Invest more intentionally in the relationships that matter to you.
- Create more than you consume.
- Give generously.
- Find what truly works for you and the life you've created for yourself.

Rewriting your story is the best adventure you will ever embark upon, and when you're approaching it from a place of grounded confidence, you will leave a lasting impact on the world around you.

When you're ready, consider the framework below to help you move through this step of your journey with focus. As someone who was (or is) very hard-headed and independent, I developed this process through a lot of trial and error as I worked to bring my vision to life. Creating this model and writing this book has brought me more joy than I ever imagined, and I'm so excited that you are along for the ride.

Intention and Exploration

As you saw above, there are numerous ways that you can share what you've learned through investing in yourself by giving back. As you step into this phase of your work, I encourage you to consider if there are times when slowing down could serve you better than keeping yourself moving full steam ahead. When you prevent your imposter self from taking up so much space on a daily basis, your true self has much more clarity and isn't trying to meet an unspoken agenda. You may find that your inner peace is more important than checking yet another personal or professional box, and you should also find joy in doing the work outlined in this chapter.

Your time is a precious resource, so going into this experience with clarity on your intention is necessary to prevent your true self from overcommitting and your imposter self from regaining control. Getting clear on the *why* and what for this work will be helpful so that you enter into this phase with solid boundaries and certainty on the time you have available to you. Here are a few writing prompts to help you as you begin:

1. What lights me up in my personal and professional lives?
2. What's something that I've never done that could be included in making someone else's life better?
3. What is important to me that doesn't involve making money?
4. What did my younger self need that wasn't available to me?

As you work through this phase of intention setting to share your Confidence Empire, challenge yourself to do something out of the box. Do something that doesn't align with your chosen profession. Try to incorporate play if possible. Don't take it (or yourself) too seriously.

After you work through the writing prompts, sit back and take inventory of any themes that you notice or anything that really sticks out to you. How does that align with what is available in your community and how you might be able to spend your time? Think about this statement:

> *I've intentionally invested in myself. I've done (and continue to do) the work. As I step out with confident and magnetic energy to share the joy and confidence I've created within myself, what feels in alignment with what I have to offer and the time available to me and will nourish my soul?*

Strategy

Now evaluate where your time outside of your personal, family, and professional commitments might be best spent.

- Do you lean into a creative project?
- Do you volunteer on a regular basis?
- Do you find someone to mentor?
- Do you write a book?
- Do you coach a youth sports team?

The possibilities are endless.

Being strategic with how you go into this stage of the work will allow you the space to keep your imposter self in check by not overextending yourself. Writing this book challenged me in ways that I never expected. Originally, I thought I could get the first draft completed in just over two months, but this was an overly ambitious goal that I didn't reach. There was more going on in my life that needed to take up space and more work that I needed to continue to do on myself. Being reminded to give myself grace while at the same time leaning into consistency taught me that life is truly about balance. Allow the process to unfold just as it's supposed to instead of trying to force something that isn't meant to happen.

As you consider how you want to share your Confidence Empire, take a very honest look in the mirror when you're considering your time commitment.

- Can you sustainably volunteer once a week, or should you start with once a month and try that out?
- Can you coach a sports team that practices twice a week and has a game every week without wearing yourself out?
- Can you commit to writing for thirty minutes or five hundred words every day, even on your days off from work? (That one was for me.)

Think about this critically, but don't allow your imposter self to paralyze you with trying to find the perfect answer. If you are finding it hard to land on your time commitment, take what you think you're able to do and cut it in half. Start there and then build up as your body, mind, and soul adjust to this addition to your schedule.

Test Run

Now that you've settled on your intention and strategy, it's time to get shit done. Think of this work like dating. You may not hit a home run at first. Prior to committing to this book, I wrote some articles for Medium. I knew that I needed to get over the fear and anxiety of having my writing available to the general public, and I needed to see if I even enjoyed writing every day, a necessity for completing a book in a reasonable timeline. Writing smaller articles helped to build the muscles of thinking in a different way, creating, and releasing the fear around hitting the publish button. As I consistently wrote on a daily basis, the idea for this book fell into my lap, and here we are. Writing became something that I looked forward to most days as it settled into my daily ritual.

Just like if you were buying a car, take a few test runs with how you go about sharing your Confidence Empire. Over my years of figuring this out, I haven't always been successful. I could easily find passion, intention, time, and desire to give back, but I failed to honor the need for alignment between all areas to be successful.

During my time in Austin, Texas, I volunteered for a bit with a non-profit dental clinic. Every other Friday, I would show up and scan paperwork into their EHR. It was necessary work, but I was bored to tears and dreaded having to show up on my assigned Fridays. After a few months, I quit showing up. I'd gone into the job hoping that I would be able to share my experience and make an impact on how the clinic was run, but I failed to commu-nicate that intention. That left me sifting through papers, pushing the scan button, and eager to find my way out of there after just a couple of hours every other week.

You don't have to enjoy the first option, or even the

first few, when you're figuring out how to share your Confidence Empire. Do the prep work and use that as a tool to maximize your time investment. As you get involved with something, feel it out. See where you feel relaxed and comfortable. When you're feeling good, think about building momentum.

- Do you commit more time to one thing?
- Do you introduce something else?
- Do you scrap all of it and go back to the drawing board?

Remember, there are no rules, so do what feels good.

Evaluate

As you lean into giving your time generously, I encourage you to spend time thinking critically about what is working and what isn't. After your test runs, spend some time thinking and/or writing about what you did and didn't enjoy. Do you want to continue down that path or try something different? Does this bring you joy, or does it feel monotonous?

Just as you would critically look at a situation with a friend or at work to determine next steps, do the same when it comes to sharing your Confidence Empire. The goal of this step of the work is to enrich your life and bring you joy in addition to helping others. Yes, this is work, but it shouldn't feel laborious.

After leaving the bedside, I quickly learned that the helping spirit I had developed as a paramedic would stay with me long after, just in a different form. When I started mentoring people, I found so much joy in creating safe spaces where they could be heard and guided in making the best decisions for themselves. I received no direct remuneration, but the joy I felt in knowing that I had helped someone break down a barrier for themselves lifted my spirit, put a smile on my face, and encouraged me to make the rest of my day the best it could be. That feeling I get when seeing someone's face light up in a moment of clarity will always motivate me to continue to move forward day by day.

As you evaluate what is working and what isn't when it comes to sharing your Confidence Empire, write down your answers to these questions:

- What do I love about this?
- What do I not enjoy?
- Do I want to continue down this path for the foreseeable future, or am I already looking for the end date?
- What would I rather be doing than this?

Course Correct

For many of us, life is full of twists and turns. Learning how to adjust to those unexpected moments is a huge part of leading a life where your true self is in control. My path has led me to many personal and career pivots. Living in three states, getting fired or laid off from jobs unexpectedly, having friends come and go from my life, and discovering the fodder that allowed my imposter self to take up too much space are just some examples of the pivots that I've faced.

Starting in my twenties, I've reinvented myself or pivoted in a big way at the beginning of every new decade. I finished paramedic school and got my license to practice when I was twenty. I left the bedside and moved to Austin, Texas, when I was thirty. I started my own business when I was forty. Throughout all of these personal and career pivots, I've had to regularly evaluate what's working and course-correct when something isn't in alignment.

Course correcting can be a great part of your journey to sharing your Confidence Empire, but it can also show up anytime you're doing the work to be the best version of yourself.

If something isn't working, evaluate why and quickly make a decision as to what your next steps will be. If you need to go down a different path, then do it. If you need to rework the rules of engagement so that more joy is solicited for you, then do it. If you need to take up more space and expand your reach, then do it. No one said you have to do the same thing every day for the rest of your life. When alignment isn't present, seek it out.

When you're doing the work, especially when sharing your Confidence Empire, and notice that something isn't working, take some space and course correct. If you did the work in the evaluate step, use what you learned from your experience and make decisions that will allow you to get back in alignment with your true self. Leave what's not working and step more fully into what feels good.

Keep Moving

The process outlined in this chapter can be used over and over again as you refine what does and doesn't work for you. As you work through the process, repeat it as often as necessary.

When you feel like stopping, don't. Keep moving. Keep on keeping on. The work never stops, unfortunately. You may step into seasons of life where the work isn't as intense or you have more space to relax and sit in the joy you've created, but to keep your imposter self in check, you have to continue to progress and allow your true self to grow. The stronger your Confidence Empire is and the more solid you are with sharing that confidence, the easier it will be to maintain the momentum you've built for your true self to lead.

Have you ever dreamed of having more success than you do today? It's possible, regardless of how you define success. Conquering success will be vastly easier when you're able to walk into a room and command the attention you deserve because you know your worth, spend your time wisely and intentionally, and respect other people's time.

When you're in alignment and doing what you're supposed to be doing, you will see that life starts to flow more easily for you. It will never be perfect, but keep doing the work to release yourself of self-doubt, perfectionism, the fear of being found out as a fraud, overworking, and thinking that success only comes to you because of luck. Your imposter self doesn't get the fuel it needs when you're in alignment and sharing your Confidence Empire. Keeping it moving allows the past to stay in the past and the present to have the necessary boundaries for your true self to shine.

A Recap of the Steps in This Chapter:

- Intention and exploration
- Strategy
- Test run
- Evaluate
- Course correct
- Keep moving

8

Thrive With Joy and Purpose

You deserve joy.

Regardless of who you are and what you have or haven't been told, you are worthy of experiencing joy on a regular basis.

Take a deep breath through your nose, hold it at the top, and sigh it out through your mouth.

Chill.

Relax.

Slow down.

How do you feel?

You've done the work, so what's next? As you heal, smooth your edges, and create space for your true self to lead, integrating all of this work into your daily life is the key to achieving a sustainable path forward. When you find what works for you, keep doing it. Focus on small, incremental improvements instead of expecting your world to be perfect from the beginning. Remember, progress is perfection.

Working through the obstacles that hold you back takes energy, but you don't want it to consume your life.

There should come a time when you can pause, sit back, and live in the joy you've created for yourself. The work will still be there when you return, but allowing yourself to be rewarded for what you've done is critical. Be proud of yourself. Be grateful for what you've accomplished. Take a vacation. Take a sabbatical. Start your own business. Take the leap that you were always scared to take.

As your imposter self loses steam, you will find that you are less risk-averse and ready to conquer challenges that you never imagined possible. When I was laid off from my last full-time job, I never imagined that I'd start my own business, write a book, and have a coaching practice. As I'm completing this book, I've been invited to teach workshops on my approach to navigating your imposter self, something I would never have imagined being in my future.

There was a time while writing this book that I didn't have much income coming in. Had my imposter self had enough energy, I would have been an anxious wreck. However, writing this book and having a coaching practice have made me feel more in alignment with my true self than I have felt in a long time. I'm not worried about the future, and that feels so good.

Capitalism teaches us that we always have to be in the machine, grinding away, getting more, keeping others happy. What about you? What do *you* want? The machine will always be there, but if you don't prioritize your true self first, you will fall into the trap of sacrificing yourself for the sake of someone or something else.

Most of us have to hustle at some point in our lives. Today's society doesn't allow for complacency if you desire anything more than mediocrity. I've been there. I worked three jobs all through my twenties. I traveled for work every week for two and a half years. I worked the sixty-hour weeks. That path allowed me to eat, put a roof over my head, and eventually put some coins in the bank. It taught me a lot about life, myself, other people, business, priorities, and my passions.

As hard as it was sometimes, I wouldn't change it for anything. It created the space for me to write this book and work for myself, but I'm also more careful how I spend my time now. During the first twenty years of my career, I had to manage through an immense amount of stress and burnout. It wasn't until I decided to go through the process outlined in this book that I realized how much was missing in the relationship I have with myself and how I care for myself. Now that I'm thriving in the alignment I've created for myself, I sit with so much joy and gratitude on a daily basis for the life I get to live.

Do the work, but also intentionally create space for the magic you've invested in. Don't let capitalism or hustle culture win. Make sure you're creating an uncrackable foundation for your true self to flourish upon.

Live Your Values

Did you complete the exercise to define your values in Chapter 4? Yes? Perfect. If not, humor me and do it right now.

Thank you. :)

One of the best ways to bask in joy on a daily basis is to bring your values into your decision-making. There is (almost) nothing better than pausing prior to making a decision, asking yourself if it aligns with your values, and then saying no if it doesn't. Maybe you'll miss out on something, maybe not, but once you have a few reps under your belt of making decisions based on your values, I bet you will find so much joy in not saying yes to everything.

I was one to give and give and give to other people until I was completely empty and unsure of what joy even was. However, coming back to my true self and finding alignment in the small things truly propels me forward on a daily basis.

Living your values is all about putting yourself first. It may not always be possible, but I challenge you to make the hard decisions and see what happens. I bet how good it feels will surprise you. Plus, when you're living your life in alignment with your values, your imposter self will struggle to find the light of day. Do you trust yourself to make the right decision? You can't simply identify your values and do nothing with them. You have to let them be your guiding light in an embodied way. Let them sit in your gut and trust your gut when it's time to make decisions.

What is Your Personal Mission Statement and Purpose?

Now that you've dismantled or reworked the toxic relationship with your imposter self, keep pressing forward with reinventing yourself.

What is your purpose?
What is your mission statement?
What are you here to do?
What is your life's work?
What is your legacy?

So many questions, I know. They're all really just different ways to contemplate the same thing: what gets you up in the morning, or what's your North Star? As divine humans, we aren't here to slog away at work for a third (or more) of our lives just to be too burned out at the end of the day or the end of our career to enjoy the simple things in life. Aligning what you do with what lights you up, what you can make money doing, and what the world needs can be the path of a lifetime. The Japanese call it *Ikigai*. You may have to shed many layers and allow your purpose to evolve over your lifetime. I sure have had to allow this to happen. If you've never intentionally spent time thinking about all of these questions or writing about them, now's your time.

When you strike the right alignment in your purpose, especially after doing the work to release control from your imposter self, you will be unstoppable. You will wake up every day feeling ready to go. Your confidence will shine. Money will flow to you. You will attract exactly what is meant for you. You will thrive.

One of my favorite ways to start the journey of developing your purpose is writing about your ideal day. My best friend, Bodhi, shared this chunk of wisdom with me a few years ago when I was in the trenches of doing my own work, and it's a really helpful tool to give your mind space to wonder and dream while also getting clear on what you're working toward.

Spend some time writing about your ideal day, what you would do if there were no rules or restrictions on money or location. Get as specific as possible; the small details matter. Write as vivid a timeline as possible from the moment you wake up until the moment you go to bed. Include how and what you feel, the physical details that stand out to you, and get into the nitty gritty on how your ideal day flows. Engage all of your senses.

As you dream into what your ideal day looks and feels like, give yourself space to wonder. Don't hold back. Once you have it all down on paper, reread it a time or two.

- What stands out to you?
- What feels attainable?
- What feels important enough that you want to start working toward it today?

Pick three things from your ideal day. Implement them into your daily practices now, or make a goal around them so that you have a path to achieving them.

Getting clear on your ideal day can help you make tweaks to the way that you live life on a daily basis, as well as give you something to work toward, but what about the work you're doing right now? What are you passionate about? What is in alignment with your true self, and how do you want to spend your time?

Now's the time for your personal mission statement, something you share with the world or hold close to your chest—it doesn't matter. This statement will provide clarity to yourself and potentially others on what you're about and why you do what you do. It can serve as a reference point when you're making decisions, especially major ones, such as with your career.

When you're ready, scan the QR at the beginning or end of this book or head over to my website (www.garet free.com) to download your free copy of my personal mission statement worksheet. The worksheet is a tool for you to craft your personal mission statement, and I'd love for you to share what you create with me.

After you live into this first version for a while, revisit your ideal day and your personal mission statement every year. New Year's Day, your birthday, a solstice, the start of springtime or fall, or an anniversary that is important to you are all good options for this.

It May Get Lonely for a Bit, but Just Wait

When you no longer need to be liked, you will become magnetic.

Setting boundaries (and holding them) is hard work and will cost you relationships, but the tradeoff is worth it in the long run. Regardless of the relationships that you have, when you start to dig deep and do the work to give your true self the space it deserves, you will have lonely moments. You will lose friends and maybe even family members. Stay the course and keep going. You may be losing the fuel that your imposter self has been happily soaking up for a long time. The discomfort is part of the process, so sit with it instead of running away.

Moving to Chicago was a big leap for me. I was ready to get out of the heat and humidity of Austin, Texas, and I wanted to live in a big city. I only knew one person when I moved to Chicago and had no idea what I was getting myself into. What initially sounded like a good idea turned into the adventure of truly stepping into my power, healing the wounds that fueled my imposter self, and giving my true self the space he deserves. There were plenty of lonely nights on my couch, drinking to the bottom of a couple of bottles of wine (oh, hey, 2020!) or partying too much and having no idea how many double vodka sodas I had ordered.

However, I kept feeling this pull to seek out something different. I knew that drinking like I was wouldn't be sustainable, and I finally took the leap to do something different. As I started to shift my life in a different direction, I found that the more I pulled inward, getting rid of distractions, the sooner I was able to find joy.

The moment I dropped the need to please others and simply be the authentic me was the moment that I realized that a happy life is possible without all the fluff. If someone or something isn't in alignment with what my true self needs in this moment, I have no shame in cutting it out and continuing with my day. If someone or something can't respect my boundaries, now I know that prioritizing my inner peace is much more important than the negative energy attempting to blackball my happiness. Setting boundaries feels hard at first until you experience the clarity that it brings.

Sitting in my life now is a party every day. The people I'm close with are aligned with me and truly add value to my life. The work I do is in alignment with my purpose and passion. I wake up most days at 5 a.m., ready to get shit done. It's all possible because I leaned into the uncomfortable yet transformative seasons of my life and soaked up all the value they provided me.

Keep Doing the Work

Keep going, especially when it feels easy. You may be thinking, *Isn't this chapter about sitting back and enjoying the life you've created for yourself?* You're right, but if you can't slow down, you need to work on that. Slowing down takes practice for a lot of people, especially doing it in an intentional way. Regardless of whether you're doing the inner work, setting boundaries, caring for your physical body, killing it at work, starting a business, reading a book, going on vacation, or meditating, do it with intention.

Every day, you have a choice to make: Do you maximize this day with the energy available to you, or do you minimize your true self and wonder why nothing ever changes? Do you continue to repeat the patterns that don't serve you, or do you strive to allow your true self the bandwidth to take up the space it deserves?

Will every day be perfect? Nope. Just yesterday, I had an off day. I was up at 5 a.m. to meditate, write my morning pages, go to the gym, write for this book, and get some other admin work done, but by the time the afternoon came, I hit a wall and spent a couple of hours on the couch, reading and doomscrolling Instagram. Then I came back and cleaned out my email and reminders list prior to making dinner. A part of me was screaming, *"Loser, get off your ass and get back to producing"* while I was at the height of my doom scroll, but thankfully, I was reminded that I had already accomplished more before 11 a.m. than a previous version of me would have ever imagined possible.

If you've picked up anything from this book, I hope that you take away the fact that perfection is an illusion and judging yourself against societal norms is not necessary. We are all divine beings and thus have the opportunity to create the life we want and deserve. Society will do everything in its power to keep you stuck, so the challenge is to persevere, do the work, and define success for yourself.

Allow Joy to be the New Normal

What is joy?

For the longest time, I thought that joy was an emotion, something that you felt. While I currently believe that is partially true, I also believe that joy is something that you create, a space you strategically seek out, a space that is created through strategic consistency.

Sitting in sorrow, suffering, or any other negative emotion is much easier to achieve.

Joy takes work. Determination. Focus.

If you're truly embarking on the journey that I've outlined in this book and committing to being a little bit better today than you were yesterday, consistently, then why not allow joy to be the norm for you? If you're doing the work to create abundance and gratitude mindsets, then cultivate the space necessary for joy. Intentionally step away from work. Intentionally spend time in nature. Intentionally spend time playing. Intentionally create.

Creating space for joy means dedicating time to rest. It means dedicating time for wonder. It means dedicating time for stillness. It means deep work without distractions. It means saying no more than you say yes. It means rearranging your life on a daily basis so that your needs are met first, prior to focusing on anyone else.

With a little bit of polish, a life full of joy is yours for the taking.

Your Turn

Take some time to reflect on these writing prompts. Put pen to paper like you've (hopefully) been doing all along.

- I am no longer available for...
- As I step into the Confidence Empire that I've built for myself, where am I going next?
- What kind of life am I building for myself now that I've done so much investment work into myself?
- How will I celebrate the wins that I've achieved so far?

If you've made it this far, I'm so proud of you. Making it to this point should prove to you that you're not broken;

you're becoming the version of yourself that has been in there all along. I'm so excited for you to keep going and create joy for yourself every day. Our time together in this book is almost wrapped up, so take a moment and congratulate yourself for getting here.

A Reminder of the Tools in This Chapter:

- Live your values
- What is your personal mission statement and purpose?
- It may get lonely for a bit, but just wait
- Keep doing the work
- Allow joy to be the new normal

Conclusion

Anytime you head out on a journey, dedication and determination are a must if you want to complete what you've started. If your imposter self has been an evergreen presence in your life, this likely isn't the first self-help book you've read, and it probably won't be the last that you pick up.

Making it this far through a book deserves a celebration in itself. I remember the days when I would make it to the halfway point of a book and lose interest because my imposter self would be in the back of my head, telling me that I didn't need anything the book had to say or that I wasn't getting any value out of it. I've since conquered that part of myself and finish most books that I start, mostly because I discovered that so many books have such great content at the end.

I hope that you've been on a journey of discovery and action with this book. We started with understanding where your imposter self comes from, why it is even something you have to deal with, and how there's nothing wrong with you if you have self-doubt, the fear of being found out as a fraud, perfectionism, the need to overwork to prove your worth, or the belief that your success is due to luck. It's okay to have these feelings, but it's also okay to do something about them. You don't need to be fixed, but can you navigate what you experience in a way that allows for more inner peace?

You can challenge your present reality so that your past (and imposter self) loses the ability to influence how you flow through life. If you're ready to do the work, dig deep, and release the hold of what happened to you, there's a joy-filled oasis ready to welcome you. Stepping into your Confidence Empire rooted in purpose will give you the foundation necessary to release the grip your imposter self has on you so that your true self can thrive.

Being a ball of self-doubt and anxiety doesn't have to be your reality. You have the power and ability to overcome your imposter self, day by day, minute by minute. Remember, progress is perfection. Just by reading this far, you're making amazing progress. Keep going!

Thank You

By reading this book, I imagine that you may have a complex past—many of us do. This book may not have all the answers you seek, but I'm so grateful that you've included my perspective on your journey to seek out what works for you.

If you've become a bit more vulnerable with yourself or others, taken the time to digest what you've read in this book, and invested in yourself to do the work, thank you. It takes courage to evolve the relationship with your imposter self. It's not lost on me the level of commitment and energy that is necessary to build your Confidence Empire as you seek out a full life that is centered on joy.

I'm so grateful to have been able to participate alongside you in this way.

Your unique story is sacred, and only you can ultimately decide what the right next step for you is, day by day. Yes, this book has been prescriptive based on my lived experience, but I encourage you to view it as a conversation between the two of us instead of an absolute doctrine.

Take the parts that work for you and try them out. Rework on the regular. Don't allow perfectionism to make you feel like you must check all the boxes as you strive toward giving your true self the space to shine it deserves. If just one thing resonates with you from this book, you try it, and it works for you, I will be so grateful for the trust you placed in me as you figure out your beautiful life.

So, What's Next?

The possibilities are endless. There are so many different directions that you can go, and I hope that you choose to thrive with confidence, joy, and authenticity. When your imposter self has too much control, it can feel like a life of confidence, joy, and authenticity is something you'll never achieve.

I challenge you to rethink that tired old narrative. This isn't a luxury; you deserve it. You may perceive that it's harder for you to achieve such a life than it is for other people, but don't let that stop you. You may never be able to erase your imposter self completely, but you can allow your relationship to evolve to a much more manageable state.

As you keep moving forward, remember that you are not alone in this work. The more you speak up, allow yourself to create, and lead with your heart, the more you will realize that everyone is on their own unique journey. What we see on the outside is only a small portion of someone's journey, so allow that to drive your curiosity instead of your judgment. Remember, everyone (including yourself) deserves grace.

If you've already started the work or if you have yet to invest in yourself, I hope that you will regularly reflect on the process provided by this book. Allow it to ease the burden of figuring out your next steps. Have you had any wins already? If so, I'd love to hear about them, and I encourage you to pause right now to celebrate your accomplishments, regardless of how big or small they may be. Leverage this momentum to keep going!

As your life evolves, I invite you to revisit this book time and time again. Anytime you're navigating through a tough season in life, this book is here as a grounding point, a compass to provide direction when you're scattered. As you regularly invest in yourself, you will feel more whole because the fear instilled by your imposter self won't be able to take up space any longer.

I would love to stay connected with you. Please visit my website, www.garetfree.com, (or scan the QR code at the beginning or end of this book), where you can find the resources mentioned in this book, sign up for my newsletter, book me as a speaker, explore coaching opportunities, join my small group masterminds, or book me for a workshop.

You don't have to struggle in silence; there's ease in sitting with community.

Additional Reading

- *The Artist's Way* by Julia Cameron
- *Fatal Conveniences* by Darin Olien
- *The Untethered Soul* by Michael Singer
- *Dare to Lead* by Brené Brown
- *Breaking Free from the Victim Trap* by Diane Zimberoff
- *Buy Yourself the F*cking Lilies* by Tara Schuster
- *Glow in the F*cking Dark* by Tara Schuster
- *The Subtle Art of Not Giving a Fuck* by Mark Manson
- *The Exceptional Presenter* by Timothy J. Koegel
- *The Body Keeps the Score* by Bessel van der Kolk

Morning Pages and Journaling Prompts

- Five things I'm grateful for today.
- How am I feeling?
- What is the one thing I can do today to make this day a success?
- My self-doubt comes from...
- What am I doing today to release myself from self-doubt?
- What does confidence feel like in this moment?
- What is my imposter self trying to protect me from?
- What will happen if I let people see my true self?
- What past experiences are preventing me from being the truest version of myself?
- What is one lie that I tell myself about my personal life?
- What is one lie that I tell myself about my professional life?
- What is a truth that I know about myself?

- What evidence do I have to know that the lies are lies?
- What evidence do I have to know that the truths are truths?
- Who benefits when I hide my true self?
- What would today feel like if I led from my values instead of fear?
- What do I feel like when I'm not trying to prove anything to anyone?
- I will display courage today by...
- What would I tell my younger self about worth and success?
- What kind of person do I want to be? What is one step that I can take today to get me there?

Acknowledgments

Life is beautiful, and I'm so grateful for every step that has led me to this moment. To anyone that has been a part of my journey until now, thank you. Regardless of how our paths crossed, you have helped shape me into who I am today which has made this book possible.

To my partner, Adam, thank you for being my biggest cheerleader through this process, for reading my drafts, giving thoughtful suggestions, and being patient. I love you.

To Roshni, thank you for being by my side through this process, for showing more enthusiasm in the book than I could muster at times, and for being a rock in my life. I love you.

To Bodhi, thank you for your friendship, love, and ear anytime I need to chat. I love you. To Stephanie and Nicole, thank you for being such amazing best friends. I love you both.

To my publisher - Zac, Cris, Rasika, Amber, Jefferson, and everyone else, thank you for making the process of publishing my first book so seamless.

To Idara, thank you for being an amazing friend and mentor who has always encouraged me to pursue my passions.

To Fred, thank you for being a stellar mentor and consistent presence in my life as I figure out my professional journey.

To Jinali, Jeena, Jaime, Travis, Carl, Melania, Mason, Emily, and Dan, thank you for the joy you bring to my life. I love you all.

Thank You For Reading My Book!

DOWNLOAD YOUR FREE GIFTS

As an additional bonus for buying and reading my book, I would like to give you a few free bonus gifts! **Scan the QR Code or head to my website - www.garetfree.com:**

Your interest in my work and this book is much appreciated, and I value your feedback as it helps me improve future versions. Leaving your invaluable feedback via a review on Amazon.com would be so appreciated. Thank you!

www.ingramcontent.com/pod-product-compliance
Lightning Source LLC
Chambersburg PA
CBHW022007080426
42733CB00007B/509